10 9 8 7 6 5

ISBN: 978-1-889102-31-3

Printed in the United States of America

Copies of this book are available from the publisher
at discount when purchased in quantity.

Emerson & Church, Publishers
15 Brook Street, Medfield, MA 02052
Tel. 508-359-0019
Fax 508-359-2703
www.emersonandchurch.com

Library of Congress Cataloging-in-Publication Data

Ahern, Tom.
  How to write fundraising materials that raise more
money : the art, the science, the secrets / Tom Ahern.
    p. cm.
  ISBN 978-1-889102-31-3 (pbk. : alk. paper)
  1. Fund raising. 2. Business writing. I. Title.
  HV41.2.A43 2007
  658.15'224—dc22
                                    2006103543

How to Write Fundraising Materials That Raise More Money

The Art, the Science, the Secrets

Also by Tom Ahern

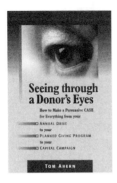

Seeing Through a Donor's Eyes
How to Make a Persuasive Case for Everything from Your Annual Drive to Your Planned Giving Program to Your Capital Campaign • 167 pp., $24.95.

"Why should I give you my hard-earned money?"

Effective fundraisers answer this essential question every time they ask for a gift. What's their secret to success? They have a winning case for support.

A case isn't some fancy argument you only develop for capital campaigns, when you're chasing millions.

Successful donor newsletters, websites, annual reports, donor acquisition programs, email, direct mail, advertising, planned giving programs, and – yes, capital campaigns, too – all have one thing in common: behind each stands a well-reasoned, emotionally satisfying case for support.

Tom Ahern, who is among America's most experienced case specialists, shares his hardest-won secrets for selling your vision and mission effectively.

Raising More Money with Newsletters Than You Ever Thought Possible
123 pp., $24.95.

Today, many organizations are raising more money with their newsletters than with traditional mail appeals.

And, after reading Tom Ahern's illuminating book it's easy to understand why. Great newsletters make the donor feel important. They use emotional triggers to spur action. They're designed in a way to attract both browsers and readers. And they don't depend on dry statistics to make the organization's case.

Transforming your newsletter into a substantial money raiser isn't that difficult. All you need to do is eliminate the Seven Fatal Flaws that Tom Ahern explores in this book.

Emerson & Church, Publishers
www.emersonandchurch.com

HOW TO
WRITE
FUNDRAISING
MATERIALS
That Raise
More Money

The ART, the SCIENCE, the SECRETS

TOM AHERN

Emerson
& Church
PUBLISHERS

About the Author

Tom Ahern, author of *Raising More Money with Newsletters than You Ever Thought Possible*, is recognized as one of North America's top authorities on nonprofit communications. He began presenting his top-rated Love Thy Reader workshops at fundraising conferences in 1999. Since then he has introduced thousands of fundraisers in the U.S., Canada and Europe to the principles of reader psychology, writing, and graphic design that make donor communications highly engaging and successful.

He founded his consulting practice in 1990. His firm specializes in capital campaign case statements, nonprofit communications audits, direct mail, and donor newsletters. His efforts have won three prestigious IABC Gold Quill awards, given each year to the best communications work worldwide.

Ahern is also an award-winning magazine journalist, for articles on health and social justice issues. He has his MA and BA in English from Brown University, and a Certificate in Advertising Art from the RI School of Design. His offices are in Rhode Island and France.

For Jane Peckham Joyaux
For the obvious reasons

Is This Book for You?

Do you consider yourself a professional writer? Can you sling strong verbs with the best of them? Do you have the emotional triggers tattooed on your frontal lobe? When somebody brings up Robert Cialdini, do you find yourself saying, "Hey, I used his scarcity idea in my last appeal!"? Did the insights of Rudolf Flesch, author of *The Art of Readable Writing*, copyright 1949, change your attitudes forever? Do you understand how advertising works? Can you find news value in the most mundane-seeming detail? Does a well-written headline cause you to pause in awe? Can you break a heart in just a few words?

An accomplished professional writer trained for fundraising and advocacy will say "yes" to pretty much all of the above. Okay, Dr. Cialdini isn't all that famous yet. But the Flesch-Kincaid readability scales are built into every copy of Microsoft Word.

If you're wondering why any of these things matter, then, yes, this book *is* for you. This book is meant for the "not-a-fulltime professional" writer, the fundraiser or advocate who wants to make more money and raise more hell...and isn't sure if her or his words are up to the task.

This book is all about trade secrets that work. If that's what you're seeking to learn and use, then, *welcome,* indeed this book is for you.

Foster, Rhode Island   Tom Ahern

CONTENTS

PREFACE

1

Why Communicate? To Spur Action

We use words to convey our messages and raise money. It's reasonable to assume, therefore, that communications are somehow about getting people to read.

But, in fact, that's not the case.

Fundraising communications are NOT about getting people to read.

Fundraising communications are about getting people to ACT ... if not immediately, then sooner or later.

■ **Action: yes. Reading: optional.**

Look at it another way. Which would you rather have, if you could only choose from these two options:

• Someone who reads your stuff but never responds?

• Or someone who doesn't read your stuff but sends you a gift?

Obviously, you'd choose the latter, as would anyone with a dollar goal to make. It's not ideal, but it pays the bills.

I bring up the distinction between reading and acting for an important reason having to do with your workload: to release you from the burden of worrying so much about writing newsletter articles, white papers, and other longer prose pieces.

The reality is, people will read very little of what you send them. They don't have time in their busy, complex lives. And most nonprofit communications aren't sufficiently interesting to win devoted readers.

This doesn't mean they don't love you, incidentally. If the people on the receiving end are donors, they *do* love you (well, they *like* you anyway). But they're time-challenged and fiercely assaulted each day by thousands of other messages.

■ They are casual readers at best

If you think of your target audience as hungry readers, you'll tend to fill your pages with prose, to satisfy their appetite.

And it will be mostly indifferent prose, it grieves me to predict.

I mean no offense. I have no doubt your writing will be factual and functional. But will it be entertaining, energetic, surprising? Will it be newsstand quality, dipped in chocolate and wrapped in 18-carat gold foil? Probably not, and that's too bad. Because entertainment, energy, and surprise make all the difference to the reader. Absent those qualities, people soon depart the page.

Keep in mind the difference between the reader you are right this moment – and the casual reader (your donors and prospects).

You're reading this page because you want to learn something to help you raise more money and develop career skills. You consider this information important to your professional success. So you're motivated to trudge on, even if you find my writing dreadful.

Casual readers aren't that motivated ... unless you're very, very good at communication skills other than long prose. This book teaches those skills.

■ Donors as action figures

I like to think of donors and prospects as action figures. And I thank a small boy in a French village for the idea.

This young fellow was playing in front of his house with his "men." Simone Joyaux, my wife, leaned down to exchange a few friendly words with him. She asked in French about his "soldiers." The boy was shy, no more than four years old. Yet he corrected her. They were not soldiers, he said. They were "le action figures."

Like the boy, I love *my* action figures: my donors and prospects. I know I can bring them to life through my deep respect for their emotional needs and for their time (as you'll also learn to do in this book). And once I bring them to life, they will win my battle for me. And in exchange I will celebrate their efforts. They are the heroes.

The fundraising industry calls that last little bit being "donor-centric." Ken Burnett calls it "relationship fundraising." It comes down to the same thing: nothing happens without someone outside your organization acting on your behalf.

■ What kinds of actions?

If communicating with donors and prospects is about causing action to happen, what kinds of actions are we talking about? A partial list would include:

- Giving to your current direct mail appeal
- Making a matching gift
- Giving to your building campaign
- Buying a membership
- Signing up for a monthly giving program
- Making a bequest
- Contributing to an endowment fund
- Volunteering
- Signing a petition
- Attending an event
- Writing a letter in support of a project
- Answering a survey
- Subscribing to your e-newsletter

… and the list goes on and on.

2

Setting Your Expectations: Be Pessimistic

Where donor communications are concerned, assume the worst. Assume they won't work.

How's that for a pep talk?

Don't get me wrong. You should be a total, fire-in-the-belly enthusiast about your organization and its mission. But getting fundraising communications to work well (i.e., bring in a sufficient financial response) is tough. You have to get a lot of technical details right. And there is one big thing you can't control: someone's time.

If you're pessimistic about results, you'll try harder. But there is a payoff: pessimists raise more money.

■ The three piles

We assume donors will pay attention to what we send them. After all, they've given us money. Obviously they care about the issue. Therefore, we assume they're motivated readers.

But are they?

At that exact moment when your communication (your appeal letter, your newsletter, your email update, your annual report) enters someone's hand and field of vision, will that person have any time to spare? Or will the person instead be busily sorting, trashing things they can safely ignore?

Like many others, I sort incoming mail into three piles:

1) Stuff I must pay attention to if I want to stay out of trouble (bills)

2) Stuff I can throw away, knowing that nothing bad will happen (virtually every other piece of direct mail)

3) Stuff I'm interested in (magazine subscriptions, catalogs I like, postcards from friends)

Note that I'm under no obligation to pay attention to donor communications. In fact, the more organizations I support, the less time I have to spend on any one. I gave them cash, I think. Isn't that enough?

■ The uncommitted

The response rate to direct mail used to acquire new donors is abysmal. One of America's best and busiest direct mail writers calls it a success if one-half of one percent of those she solicits respond to her appeal. In others words, 99.5 percent of the people who receive her appeals throw them away, probably unread.

Which is why I urge you: be a pessimist. Assume even your donors will ignore you most of the time. You'll be close to the truth. Why? Not because they suddenly dislike you. On the contrary: they are your truest of true believers. They've sent you a check in the past to prove it.

But they're short of time. Which means they won't commit easily to reading your materials. That's a key concept in communications: your donors and prospects are always uncommitted.

Nobody has enough time these days. And if someone does have a few minutes of downtime, will they want to spend it on your materials? They don't know. They're not sure. They're uncommitted.

Most days we have on our hands a small amount of what might be called "disposable attention." It's similar to disposable income: it's what left over, once you've paid attention to everything else demanding your time (your finances, your job, your family, your projects, your chores, your favorite book, the newspaper).

You can spend your disposable attention on anything you want. Inevitably, you spend it on things that interest you, a topic so important it gets its own chapter.

3

The Almighty Predisposed

Who are "the predisposed" and why do they matter?

The predisposed are your donors of tomorrow. Your job is to seek them out. The predisposed are those who intrinsically agree with your mission and vision. Some fundraisers call them "suspects."

The predisposed might not know your organization's name yet. They might not know anything about what you do. They might not have given your issue any special thought, for that matter.

But when they hear what you have to say, in their hearts they know you're right. And therefore they are likely to make a gift.

Quick example:

Like you, I breathe air and drink water to stay alive. That fact makes me automatically predisposed to care when I hear about an air or water problem. If the mission of your organization is to solve my air or water problem, then I am predisposed to support you.

You simply need to put something in front of me that will penetrate my inertia and convince me (make it quick, please) that my money, given to you, could make a difference. (Of course, it's not a simple task at all. But that's in part why you're reading this book.)

4

Making It Interesting (Mandatory)

Let us now praise extraordinary insights, this one courtesy of Howard Luck Gossage (1917-1969), "a man who hated advertising," it's said, yet was inducted into the Advertising Copywriters Hall of Fame.

Celebrated ad pioneer David Ogilvy called Gossage, "the most articulate rebel in the advertising business," a man who felt "advertising was too valuable...to waste on commercial products...that it justified its existence only when it was used for social purposes" (i.e., for good causes).

Here's what the estimable Mr. Gossage had to say, "The real fact of the matter is that nobody reads ads. People read what interests them, and sometimes it's an ad."

And sometimes it's your direct mail solicitation ... or the cover story on your donor newsletter ... or that email alert your organization just sent.

In each case the decision to read or not to read your stuff will come down to one thing: Is a person interested in what you're saying and/or showing? Since this is a vitally important principle, let me repeat. Your donors and prospects are under no obligation to pay attention. If you don't somehow interest them, they won't read what you send.

■ How to interest people: A checklist

So how *do* you interest people? Here's a checklist of some things I consider when I write for donors or prospects:

Am I being "donor-centric" enough?

• Have I said what amazing things the organization did (or would do) with their gifts? Did I mention worthwhile results? Real accomplishments?

• Did I link these accomplishments back to charitable giving?

• Did I celebrate the donor as the hero? (In other words, did I say in some fashion over and over, "This good work would not be possible without your help.")

• Did I talk about the organization's cost efficiency? (In surveys, donors often say that they believe charities are poorly run. And this already high level of skepticism is increasing.)

Am I taking advantage of human psychology?

• Am I telling (and showing) people things they

don't know? That is, does my information have news value? Is it unique or innovative? Are my photos surprising in some way?

• Is it bold, passionate? (Not bland, predictable, or boring.)

• Am I aiming for the heart? Have I included plenty of emotional triggers (fear, anger, greed, exclusivity, scarcity)? *See chapter 23.*

• Is the word "you" used often?

• Is the tone conversational rather than formal?

• Am I making it easy for skimmers, flippers, and browsers to glean information? If, for instance, someone reads just the headlines, will the person still understand my key messages?

• Is the publication as a whole a quick read? Am I writing short sentences? Am I using action verbs? Have I eliminated jargon?

• Since anecdotes are the fastest way to explain anything, am I using anecdotes to illuminate our most pressing issues?

• Am I using my statistical evidence like a spear, to make a single important point?

• Can I use testimonial anywhere, to inspire the faithful and calm the doubters?

• People want to act. Have I made at least one offer they can respond to?

5

Secret to Response: The Offer is King

The purpose of an offer is simple: it gives the reader a reason to respond to you right now.

Every day, you probably weigh dozens of offers yourself.

In every catalog you receive, each item is an offer. When you buy lunch, "Would you like fries with that?" is an offer. When you visit a website, pretty much anything you can click on, including the word "more", is in fact an offer.

But wait, there's more: The richer you make your offer, the stronger the response. An irresistible offer overcomes hesitance and inertia. That's why challenges and matching gift campaigns often boost fundraising income significantly – people want to take advantage of a limited-time offer. We absolutely, positively adore multiplying our gift to a favorite charity ... without in fact spending a penny more. And we don't want to

Special Offer...

The Hidden Zoo Tour

Take our special "behind the scenes" V.I.P. (W.L.A.) Tour*
Spend a little time with us on your own personal, expert-guided tour of
the Hidden Zoo...and we guarantee you'll be talking about it to everyone! (Now you know our secret purpose!) To schedule your visit, call
director Jack Mulvena at 401-941-3910.

*Very Important People (Who Love Animals)

The Campaign to Make Roger Williams Park Zoo Exceptionally Great (Again).

"Insider" tours are a great way to make lifelong friends for your group.
For its $35 million capital campaign, Roger Williams Park Zoo (Provi-
dence, RI) devoted a page in the case statement to its eye-opening and
exciting V.I.P. tour offer.

miss the chance.

Direct marketing professionals say, "The offer is king." They mean: Find the right offer, and response pours in.

Conversely, without any offers, expect no response. I mention this because I see, for example, plenty of donor newsletters containing no offers at all. (And you wonder why no one ever calls or writes?)

■ Don't bury your offer

Making an offer ("Call this number for more information") at the end of a long article guarantees that most people will miss it.

Celebrate every offer you make. Make it big, bold, easy to spot.

■ What's in an offer?

Remember: the purpose of offers is to stimulate response. And you're probably *already* making offers. Each appeal letter you send is an offer, for instance. Essentially you're saying: "Send us a gift, and we'll make the world a better place in your name."

Other common offers from fundraisers include:
- "For more information"
- An invitation to join an exclusive society such as a President's Circle
- An invitation to an event
- A free, informative brochure
- Free membership

- Discounted membership ("Your family membership entitles you to unlimited visits...")
- A member card
- A free subscription to your electronic or printed newsletter
- Special, timely updates from the president
- A free calendar of upcoming events and shows
- Discounts for advance purchase of tickets
- Special member-only previews
- Matching gift campaigns
- The ease and convenience of giving online
- A naming opportunity
- A behind-the-scenes tour
- A cow (see below)

■ Heifer's four-footed offers: Making the intangible real

Heifer Project International (Little Rock, AR; founded 1944; www.heifer.org) has a simple plan for ending world hunger: they give poor people livestock that produce food and income, as well as training in how to keep the animals healthy and reproductive. It's the "teach a man to fish" philosophy in action.

In a recent year, Heifer raised roughly $45 million from individuals for its work in 51 countries. How? In part, through offers in what it calls "the most important gift catalog in the world."

The Heifer catalog offers donors the chance to buy an animal suitable for farming: a water buffalo, a llama, chickens, a flock of ducks, even honey bees. If you can't afford an entire pig this year ($120), you can buy a *share* of a pig for as little as $10. Heifer even has a gift registry, if you're looking "for a more meaningful way to celebrate events such as weddings, anniversaries, birthdays, graduations, and holidays." There is an interesting communications strategy behind these offers. Heifer has taken something fairly intangible (its mission, and the donor's hope that "my gift will make the world a better place") and turned it into something quite tangible: a pig or other bountiful creature put into a person's needy hands. "Nothing's more satisfying than finding exactly the right solution to a problem," says Heifer. "That's the good feeling you get when you give an Asian subsistence farmer a water buffalo."

I can see it. I can almost smell it.

Now in truth you are not buying a specific animal for a specific family in a specific country. Nor are you benefiting a specific child with your gift to a development agency such as Plan International, to give another example. The child's entire community benefits from your gift.

Heifer makes this clear in the fine print: "The prices in this catalog represent the complete livestock gift of a quality animal, technical assistance and training. Each purchase is symbolic and represents a contribution to the entire mission of Heifer International. Donations will be used where needed most to help struggling people." So, yes, it's a symbolic purchase. But the bottom line is, somebody somewhere still gets a cow.

The lesson is this: when you can make your mission more tangible, it's easier for the prospect to imagine the result. In turn, when prospects can easily imagine the result, they're more likely to become donors. They can see the mission in their mind's eye. It's real. It's not a promise. It's a promise *fulfilled*.

Heifer International has made its mission tangible through livestock offers. What can you offer that will tangibly symbolize your mission? A university selling $2 million endowed chairs offers pictures of 20 assorted chairs, different styles from different periods, throne to recliner, wittily chosen. Each has a space on it labeled, "Your name here."

What's your tangible symbol?

6

Why Your Fundraising Communications Fail to Get the Results You Want

There's "Built to Last." There's "Built for Success." And then there's "Built to Fail." Here are six ways you guarantee poor results in your fundraising communications. And they have nothing to do with the quality of your writing or design:

Reason #1: You don't target your audience narrowly enough.

How narrowly? Fundraisers, at a minimum, need to recognize that donors, prospects, and suspects are three distinct target audiences. Here are my working definitions:

• **Donors.** *Authentic* donors are those who have given you at least two gifts. Why two? Because the renewal rate for first-time contributors is abysmally low. In my book, a one-time donor is still a prospect. Many fish landed during acquisition campaigns flop right back out of the boat and swim away to some other charity's lure. Many first-time gifts aren't investments in your mission. They are impulse purchases (disaster relief) or one-offs (memorial gifts).

It's premature (and dangerously complacent) to immediately label first-time givers "donors" when, in reality, there's a 70 percent chance they won't make a second gift, as experts such as Mal Warwick warn. Not only do you have to acquire first-time donors, you have to *re*-acquire them for that second gift.

An authentic donor has shown a commitment to your mission, expressed through multiple gifts.

• **Prospects.** Prospects are those who have shown some interest in your mission. Maybe they've taken a giant step forward and given an initial gift. Maybe they've merely asked to join your mailing list.

Prospects include all "lapsed donors": LYBUNTs (those who gave "last year but unfortunately not this") and SYBUNTs ("some year but unfortunately not this"). A foundation, for example, turns from a suspect into a prospect when it responds to your letter of inquiry with an invitation to submit a full proposal.

• **Suspects.** Suspects are just that: people you suspect *might* yield a gift, though you have no proof yet that they're really interested. For some reason they look promising.

If you're a community hospital, for example, residents within a certain radius might qualify as suspects since they're most likely to end up in your emergency room. If you're a college, all the alumni who have never responded are definitely suspects (not prospects).

Putting someone on your mailing list without her or his consent makes that person a suspect, not a prospect.

Each of these target audiences responds to a different set of messages. Consider:

• Donors already sort of love you. Prospects, though, still wonder whether you're *worth* loving. Suspects scarcely know you exist.

• Donors are a tiny bit skeptical: they need just a dash of reassurance. Prospects are furiously skeptical: they need big second helpings of reassurance. Suspects assume you're not worth their time and money until you convince them otherwise.

• Donors respond because they believe their investments in your mission make a difference to the world. Their gifts enhance their feelings of self-worth, and sometimes their gifts are large. Prospects respond because you've diligently worked at winning their trust. They'll risk a small amount. Suspects respond, if at all, because you've made an offer they can't pass up.

And that's just for starters. Now let's look at "segmentation."

Marketers have known for decades that segmentation is the secret to increased sales and profitability. Segmentation breaks down broad audiences (the mythic "everyone") into smaller, more manageable target audiences. Each segment includes just those people who share certain traits.

There are two types of traits you can work with: "demographic" and "psychographic."

Demographic traits are the basics. They include characteristics such as age, sex, income, educational level, number of children, or zip code.

Psychographic traits (also known as "lifestyle" traits) dig deeper. Psychographic traits include values, beliefs, attitudes, and interests — as well as revealing evidence: what people buy, what they read, how they vote, where they make their charitable gifts.

Rent a mailing list by household income, and you're dealing with demographics. Rent a mailing list of subscribers to a certain magazine, and you're dealing with psychographics.

A keen understanding of segmentation helps you avoid wasteful, expensive mistakes. You'll tilt at fewer windmills. Face it: if you're a zoo, don't expect to raise much money from childless couples. Although accredited zoos have a serious secondary mission (keeping breeding populations of endangered species alive and well), zoos primarily exist to entertain and educate kids. Zoos are smart to target parents. Segmentation forces you to sharpen your message. And it helps you find the promising segments and skip those who are unlikely to be predisposed (e.g., the abovementioned childless couples).

If you're a fundraiser who does face-to-face solicitations, you're already well acquainted with segmentation. A face-to-face solicitation is a textbook example of targeting and tailoring your message: in that meeting, you respond to the peculiar interests and concerns of just one person.

Bottom line: there is no such thing as "the general public," and effective messages do not come in "one size fits all."

Reason #2: You don't know what your BIG message is.

You don't know what you really want to say to your target audience. You don't have "The Message" clear in your own head.

What is "The Message"?

It's your BIG message, the message you MUST get into your donors' and prospects' minds to win their support.

• For a university eager to improve its reputation for academic excellence, the most important message for major-gift prospects was this: "We're under-endowed. And that's holding us back."

- For a community hospital in Massachusetts, the number-one message for local donors and prospects was: "We give you outstanding medical care close to home, particularly in cardiology. Which is good, because our region has the highest incidence of heart disease in the state."

- For HousingWorks RI, a massive coalition, the number-one message for voters and their legislative representatives was this:

"Rhode Island has a housing crisis. Our economic development experts say the crisis is hurting the state's competitiveness for new business. The crisis is due to a housing shortage. We simply do not have enough homes, and there are too many people competing for them. People with modest incomes (the bulk of the state's workforce) can't afford these inflated prices, so they lose their shot at decent housing in a good community. We have to find a way around anti-development obstacles. We have to build more houses and apartments that are both affordable and high quality."

Notice that the last example of "The Message" is quite long. It takes several steps to argue its case.

That's okay. "The Message" is not a sound bite. It's actually more of a goal: "This message is the one idea we want to plant firmly inside the heads of our target audience. When the members of our target audience hear and understand this message, we're much more likely to gain their support."

Then there's the opposite approach, the one that leads to failure. Instead of sending the same BIG message over and over, you send lots of different messages. Instead of amassing conviction over time by returning to the same BIG message from lots of different angles (which is the secret to keeping "The Message" fresh and interesting), you serve up lots of different messages that aren't mutually reinforcing and lead nowhere special.

Choose one message for each target audience and beat that message to death for a few years. That's how you get results. Which brings me to...

Reason #3: You don't repeat your messages often enough.

How many messages are *you* sending out? How many times for each? The answers are likely to be, in order, "Too many. And too few."

Repetition until you are blue in the face is the secret to success in advertising and every other form of consumer communications including fundraising.

Marketers cite the "rule of seven" (or 10 or 12, the numbers vary) with superstitious fervor. That rule states that you must bring to the same target audience the same message at least seven times in an 18-month period in order for that message to penetrate.

Reason #4: You don't have real goals.

Characterized by: (1) your goals can't be measured

because they're not easily quantified; (2) your goals aren't monetary in an obvious sense; (3) you don't define your target audiences narrowly; (4) you don't analyze how each target audience get its information. Instead, you chase soap bubbles: vague, pseudo-goals such as "raising community awareness."

A real goal reads something like, "Adding more than 500 millionaires with an interest in community philanthropy to our house mailing list." Every goal should be concrete, measurable, achievable, and worth doing. (And, yes, that goal of gathering in hundreds of new millionaires was real and achieved, in Rhode Island of all places, the smallest state in America.)

Reason #5: You think "bland" is the safe choice.

It isn't. To paraphrase ad great David Ogilvy, you'll never bore anyone into paying attention...or sending you that first check. Marketing (and the peculiar sub-branch known as "fundraising") is neither for the meek nor the timid. You *have* to be BOLD to capture a person's attention in today's hyperactive messaging environment (though please note: "capturing attention" isn't the same as being offensive). Boldness has another advantage: it's how your organization can overcome advertising budgets too limited to purchase high levels of repetition.

Reason #6: You have unreasonable expectations.

You're optimistic, not pessimistic. Low yields make you nervous. Instead, you hope for blockbusters. You don't understand that each new fundraising channel you open will likely contribute just a trickle. Take heart, though: together, those trickles will converge over time into a mighty river of support.

7

Writing Your Strategy

Behind every profitable ad campaign stands a document known variously in the industry as the "advertising strategy" or "creative brief" or "strategy statement."

This written strategy answers critical questions. Who is the target consumer? What is the unique benefit of the product? What are the values (or personality) of the brand? Why are we doing this? What are we trying to accomplish with this ad? What will the ad cause the target audience to think, feel, or do?

The purpose of a written strategy is to get everyone on the same page, quite literally. Writers, designers, client, account executive: you want everyone involved in this expensive process to be headed in the same direction. It produces a better result. It avoids conflicts.

■ What this means to you

Fundraising materials are no different than other forms of advertising. If anything, fundraising materials face an even tougher job of persuasion, because they're trying to sell the intangible: the feeling of doing good. With a written strategy you guarantee that copywriters, designers, staff and board all share the same understanding of what your organization hopes to achieve. Having a mutually understood goal written out for each direct mail appeal, event invitation, campaign case statement, donor newsletter (and other initiative), will avoid conflicts and produce better results. It will streamline your review and approval process. Which will in turn make your organization more efficient.

In case I haven't yet been emphatic enough, let me be crystal clear: *Writing a strategy is not an option. It's essential to your success.*

■ Asking the right questions

There are three preliminary questions you'll need to answer in order to write a strategy:

1. Who is your specific, target audience?
2. What do you want that target audience to do once they've encountered your communication?
3. What's in it for them if they do the action you're proposing?

Once you have answers to these three baseline questions, you can write a strategy. It's that simple. And the formula is short and sweet. Just fill in the blanks in the following statement:

This [enter name of communication item] will convince [enter name of target audience] that [enter name of action you want them to take] could [enter name of benefit].

Here are two strategies that followed this formula to produce successful fundraising brochures:

• [*For a community symphony*] This brochure listing our upcoming season's musical offerings *[the communication item]* will convince music lovers in the Plymouth, MA region *[the target audience]* that buying a season subscription *[the action you want them to do]* will give them enjoyable, exciting, professional-level musical experiences without driving to Boston *[what's in it for them]*.

• [*For a new "special interest" fund at a community foundation*] This case statement *[the communication item]* will convince feminists of both genders *[the target audience]* that supporting the Women's Fund with their gifts *[the action you want them to do]* will help level a very unfair playing field in Rhode Island *[what's in it for them]*.

■ **Other questions to ask**

Good, useful, profitable communications are all about asking questions first. Here are a few more you need to ask before you start creating:

• What doesn't the reader know? (Safe answer: everything.)

- Why should the reader care about us, our mission, our accomplishments or any other detail which you're considering including?
- You want them to do something, right? How will they respond? What's the mechanism?
- What's the first thing people will see and read? (You'll want to start with a hook of some kind – visual, verbal or both – to guarantee their attention.)

8

On the Delicate Subject of Committee and Board Approvals

Moments like this happen quite often in my workshops.

I'll mention something that industry professionals pretty much all agree on. The perfect example: Repeated tests find that four-page letters used to acquire new donors typically out pull one-page letters, all else being equal. Counter-intuitive? Absolutely. But much of direct mail practice seems at first glance contrary to common sense.

A hand goes up. It's a worried query from an attendee who smells trouble ahead. "My board chair says he throws away four-page letters whenever he gets one. So he'll only approve one-pagers. What should I do?"

Show him this chapter.

Hope that reason prevails.

Be well trained. Know what you're talking about. And realize that his opinion is entirely personal and applies nowhere outside his head.

Humans have this bad habit of generalizing from the particular. "I don't like it" gets all too easily confused with "*No one* will like it." It's bad logic and even worse statistics.

■ Beware who gets approval rights

With fundraising communications, there are only two states of being: "I know what I'm doing" or "I don't."

Professional staff members are supposed to be the in-house authorities. They *should* know what they're doing.

They either have the technical expertise themselves to write and design fundraising materials ... or they hire that expertise from a freelancer, consultant, or vendor.

Or they have on hand expert books that demonstrate how to do these things the right way. I can't think of any topic in fundraising or advocacy communications that can't claim a book written by a credible expert.

It's unusual, though, to find that kind of professional expertise in board or committee members (or in many executive directors, for that matter).

Yet we often cede the weighty responsibility of

"blessing" fundraising communications to higher authorities: boards, committees, the executive director. That's irresponsible. Uninformed opinions and second-guessing can, without malice or intent, easily ruin competent work and undermine your ability to raise money. When untrained people have the final say on what goes out the door, you run a serious risk. Let's look at why.

■ Instincts aren't enough

No one is born with an instinct for correctly judging direct mail.

Even long-time direct mail professionals, people with hundreds of properly conceived and executed efforts in their memory banks, admit they're never quite sure if a new appeal will succeed or not. Which is exactly why these same professionals test so religiously and rigorously.

And that's just direct mail. There's a body of knowledge behind *every* professional communications piece, whether it's an annual report, a newsletter, a case statement, an emailed appeal, or a website. Acquiring that body of knowledge requires training.

Effective fundraising communications – solicitation letters, promotional ads, case statements and the rest – are in my opinion 99% science and 1% art. If my assessment is right, training and experience, clearly, make all the difference.

An untrained person might (unlikely, but possible)

guess a few things right out of the 25 basic things one needs to know to succeed in the tough business of communicating with strangers. But those many other mistaken guesses will kill your chances.

■ Non-professionals use the wrong criteria

Inventor Henry Ford once observed, "If we'd asked the public what they wanted, they would have said, 'faster horses.'"

That profound remark also neatly makes a point germane to our discussion: People work with what they know. Ask an untrained person for an opinion, and you'll get one, particularly if it's about the written word. But the context and references on which that opinion is based will be personal, not professional.

When an untrained person says, "I like it," it's a matter of taste.

When a trained person says, "I like it," it's a matter of judgment, using recognized and proven criteria.

In a professional approval process, personal taste is irrelevant and often misleading because it tends to favor the safe over the bold.

■ The problem with committees

Though I've known exceptions, committees, by their very nature, tend to make things worse.

They feed each other's doubts. They're protective of the organization's image. They try to sand off all the edges and find a solution everyone agrees is inoffensive. But during the "blandifying" process, they often also scrub away the interesting bits: the bold, the controversial, the crazy surprises.

BIG mistake.

Advertising legend, David Ogilvy, once wrote, "You cannot *bore* people into buying your product; you can only *interest* them in buying it."

Sound advice, widely applicable. You cannot *bore* people into paying attention. You cannot *bore* people into becoming supporters. You cannot *bore* people into acting on your behalf.

Ask any good marketer: Bold outsells bland every time. And that goes for fundraising, too. In the bowels of the direct mail industry, there's even a belief that if no one complains, you haven't pushed hard enough. If no one calls your office to say, "I just got your latest fundraising appeal. How dare you show a picture like that!", then you're not close enough to the edge and your income will suffer.

Unfortunately, that's not how humans on committees tend to behave. Risk aversion is more likely the order of the day. In his classic, *Confessions of an Advertising Man*, Ogilvy flashes this dismissive rhyme:

> *Search all the parks in all your cities;*
> *You'll find no statues of committees.*

But, as I say, I have known exceptions.

9

What is Branding, Really?

Your brand is not your logo. (That's your trademark.) Nor is your brand your so-called "corporate identity" (the consistent use of visual elements like trademarks, on everything from stationery to vehicles). Nor is your brand your product or service.

Your brand is how your target audience feels about you.

"A brand," writes Marty Neumeier, "is a person's gut feeling about a product, service, or company." Why listen to Marty? Because his business is building enormously successful brands for clients like Apple and HP. And he shares his insights in a much-praised, finish-it-on-a-plane-ride book, *The Brand Gap*.

"[A brand is] a GUT FEELING," he writes in his introduction, "because we're all emotional, intuitive beings, despite our best efforts to be rational. It's a PERSON'S gut feeling, because in the end the brand is defined by individuals, not by companies.... Each person creates his or her own version of [your brand].... When enough individuals arrive at the same gut feeling, a company can be said to have a brand. In other words, a brand is not what YOU say it is. It's what THEY say it is."

■ **Objective: Trust. It starts with the phone.**

One of the most important goals of branding is to build trust in your target audience: prospects and donors, in our case.

Some of this you can plan.

If, for instance, on your website, you correctly anticipate the most pressing questions of your target audience and deliver frank, forthright answers, your organization will seem intelligent and trustworthy.

If, for instance, you frequently celebrate the donor in your publications ("It starts with you. Without your gifts, we couldn't begin to do our work."), your organization will seem grateful and empowering. (See how easy this branding stuff is?)

There are some other aspects of brand-building in your control — if you care to bother. A key one: be especially conscious of what happens at points of contact between your organization and your target audience.

One community foundation director retitled her receptionist position, "Our Director of First Impressions." Brilliant! This ED knows that much of her foundation's brand hangs by a thread: the voice, training, and helpful attitude of the person answering the phone. Yet how many organizations leave this critical contact to chance? How many grudging, low energy, suspicious-sounding people perform as "Director of First Impressions"? I encounter them all the time.

10

Warning: You Are An Intrusion, Too

Every day thousands of messages aim for your eyes and ears, and through those points of entry, your heart and mind ... via web, TV, radio, newspapers, magazines, roadside advertising, faxes, flyers pinned to bulletin boards, bumper stickers, labels on bottles and cans ... and, even more personally, mail, email, and phone.

You are besieged by voices eager to get a piece of you: your time, your loyalty, your money.

Is it any wonder your defenses are up?

Nonprofit communications don't enjoy any special exemptions. Your materials, particularly your fundraising materials, are part of the onslaught. You are an intrusion, too. And each item your organization sends is guilty until proven innocent.

Guilty of what? Guilty of wasting the reader's time

with material that hopes to serve *your* purpose (raise money or rally support) but doesn't interest the reader ... as if those were two unrelated things.

Early in this book, I urged you to be pessimistic when communicating to prospects and supporters. *Don't* expect good results. It's a paradox, but it works in your favor: the less optimistic you are, the more you achieve. Why? Because as a card-carrying communications pessimist and all-around smart person, you'll end up trying harder to do the one thing that's necessary to be effective: interest your readers.

How do you interest them?

In Chapter 4 of this book, I offered a checklist. It was a quick skim of the topic.

Now we'll dive deeper to explore in detail the fascinating question of how to write to strangers. And how practical psychology helps you capture and hold the interest of prospects and supporters.

11

What Interests Donors

Donors have special interests. Here's a short list of things they care about deeply:

- Your accomplishments. *What did you do with my money? Are you making a difference?*
- Your vision. *If I choose to give you more money, what amazing things could you do with it?*
- Recognition. *Are donors like me vital to your work?*
- Your efficiency. *Can I trust you with my money?*

■ In the lead: Accomplishments

Of these four interests, the most critical will be, without doubt, your accomplishments.

Your donors are your investors. They've invested in your specific mission, hoping you'll change for the better a piece of the world they care about. It is your responsibility to keep your investors well informed of your progress. We all grew up on the "Little Engine

That Could." The little engine that can't deserves no further support. To put it baldly, investors want to back winners.

■ Linked to accomplishment: Need

First the good advice, from Hal Malchow, veteran of dozens of political fundraising campaigns, "...you'll raise far more money with news of a setback that leaves you in desperate need and your mission yet to be accomplished." Than you will, it should be said, if what you report is how great things are going.

Don't get me wrong. You *should* celebrate your triumphs. But always leave room for accomplishing more, if only you had more resources. Your gains as an organization don't wipe out all the community's needs. Give your true believers (i.e., donors) plenty of opportunities to renew their faith in you, by investing again. Lean on them. Show them your need.

And I'll reinforce that with one piece of anecdotal evidence.

We were writing newsletters for a Boys & Girls Club. When our front-page headlines emphasized triumph but neglected to mention need, giving in response to that issue fell. When our next issue came out, our front page emphasized triumph yet also boldly stated, "But we can do more, if we have your help." Gifts in response jumped back to earlier, higher levels.

Always reserve a space for need at the front of your donor communications.

■ Recognition: It's more than a list of names

Every organization publishes its list of donor names with a big "Thanks!" And they believe they're pretty much done with recognition.

That kind of name recognition is nice. It's necessary. But it's not sufficient. It fails to nourish the main psychological root cause why donors remain steadfast and generous: the desire to be needed.

Donors want to feel they're important to the attainment of your mission. They want to feel they authored some change in the world when they made the decision to believe in you and write you that first check.

Tell donors how important they are to your mission. Be gloriously "donor-centric." In the next chapter you'll learn how easy that is.

■ Vision: Complications not required

Of course, you need "today dollars" to keep the lights on and your mission alive. But donors also want to know where you're headed. What are your organization's dreams for tomorrow?

Raise tomorrow's dollars today, by preparing your donors and prospects for the goals ahead. For instance, write about the problems you can't change yet, but wish to change within another five years, if donors choose to fund you.

Visions don't have to be complicated, either. The greatest visionaries in the world are farmers. They see a bountiful harvest in their minds months before it appears. In other words, not every vision requires a strategic plan to back it up.

■ **Tape this to the inside of your forehead: It's not about funding your agency.**

Fundraising is not about funding your agency.

It's about realizing the donor's dreams and needs.

They don't support [insert your name here]. They support your mission and vision, because those mean something to the donor.

And there's one other small problem: they don't necessarily trust you all that much either, though they would like to.

Never stop talking about how efficient you are as a business enterprise. Donors need to hear it, because ... well, because they assume otherwise. They assume you're inefficient. One UK study found that donors expected charities to spend (misspend, really) 65% of every gift on administration and fundraising, rather than on program expenses. You must counter those incorrect assumptions repeatedly. They corrode donor loyalty.

12

Being Donor-Centric

Being "donor-centric" is remarkably easy.

You can do it successfully in your very next solicitation letter, newsletter, e-news update, brochure, website makeover, program book, speech, press release, grant application, or annual report.

Simply learn to distinguish between the "donor-optional" and the "donor-centric" points of view.

• *Donor-OPTIONAL* point of view: "We did this. We did that. We were amazing. Oh, by the way, thanks."

• *Donor-CENTRIC* point of view: "With your help, all these amazing things happened. And without your help, they wouldn't have."

Note the essential difference.

In the donor-optional statement, your organization takes all the credit for the accomplishments. The donors are recognized as interested bystanders, good for a gift but that's all.

In the donor-centric statement, the donor is moved center stage. The glory-hogging "we" disappears. Instead, you place the responsibility for your organization's success squarely on the donor's shoulders.

Moving the responsibility onto donors' shoulders can be a highly profitable shift. Donors feel good when they know they've made something worthwhile happen. They'll seek that good feeling again and again by making additional gifts.

Writing in a donor-centric way isn't idle flattery, in case you wondered. Donor-centric communications sincerely celebrate the *actual*, and *potential*, contributions donors make to your mission and vision.

■ For example: Rewriting a headline to be more donor-centric

Here's the original headline and "deck" (also known as a subtitle) from the newsletter of the Southwest Mental Health Center in San Antonio, Texas; with permission:

> Why do kids come here? They need help to get safe, work through traumatic experiences, find their place in the world – to get back on the right track
>
> **One thing our children don't lack is hope**

Here's the proposed donor-centric rewrite:

When kids come to us, their desperate lives might look hopeless. But with your help, there's always hope available at Southwest Mental Health Center.

Your support of the Center helps "crisis kids" like these

What's the difference? The major sin of the first headline-and-deck combo: It's all about "us." The donor's nowhere to be found.

The second headline is set up using a formula that guarantees the donor is never out of the picture. The formula has three parts.

1) In the deck, where we have elbow room, we dramatize the problem.

2) Same place, we position ourselves as the solution, thanks to the donors.

3) In the headline, the biggest type on the page, we shift a large chunk of the responsibility for healing these "crisis kids" onto the donors' shoulders.

The emphasis on "hope" in both versions is there for a reason. Hope is one of the dozen or so emotional triggers experts know yield higher response rates from donors and the predisposed.

■ Being donor-centric when donors are a small percentage of your income

If your organization receives 98 percent of its funding from government contracts or insurance reimbursements, and donors contribute a "mere" two percent, can you seriously make the case that donors are crucial to your mission without stretching the truth?

Often you can. Try changing the frame of reference from "big picture" to "close-up." If your donors seem like small fish in a big financial pond, reduce the size of the pond. Focus tightly on a single area where charity matters a lot. Here's a perfect example, again from the Southwest Mental Health Center newsletter:

It costs $1,000 to hospitalize
a child in crisis for two days...

How can my $25 gift make a difference?

Mental health services aren't cheap. And even when health plan benefits cover inpatient treatment, those reimbursement dollars pay only for psychiatric and clinical services. There are so many things insurance just won't pay for...

• *Haircuts and hairbrushes* for children who need help learning to groom themselves

• *Books and inexpensive outings* for children who need help learning to use their leisure time constructively

• *Sometimes extra clothing* for a court-committed child who may spend 90 days in our care without a parent to bring a smile or a change of underwear.

...That's how your $25 gift will make a difference. You don't have to be wealthy to have a practical, everyday impact in the life of a child.

NOTE: "Deck" is the editorial term for what civilians call a "subhead." It is the bigger type juxtaposed to the headline, the biggest type, and before the article. There *are* subheads. They appear in the body of the article, to break up dense columns of prose. Feature stories almost always need a deck (or two) as well as a headline, to properly reveal the significance of a story. A deck and a headline are inseparable; they are a unit; they are a duo that together tell the story.

13

Communicating on All Four Wavelengths

Communications are all about the mind ... and *only* about the mind. Keep that in mind.

Your website, your direct mail appeals, your donor newsletters, your grant applications are all trying to score in the same arena, the *cranial* arena. When you get right down to it, it's just *your* brain trying to influence someone *else's* brain.

Fortunately, we know quite a bit about brains and their habits. Contemporary marketers owe many of their triumphs to the discoveries of psychoanalysis and neuroscience. Where would modern public relations be, for instance, without the theories of Sigmund Freud?

Freud's nephew, Edward Bernays, was a publicist in New York City. As a young man trying to make his name, Bernays adapted his Uncle Sigmund's insights to mold public opinion in favor of bacon, cigarettes, soap, and fluoride in municipal drinking water. A new age of consumer manipulation had emigrated from a Viennese clinic. Freudian-inspired methods earned Bernays famous clients like Procter & Gamble and the titles "father of public relations" and "father of spin."

Swiss psychiatrist Carl Jung, Freud's one-time collaborator, also plays a role in effective communications. Vestiges of Jung's theories of "psychological types" now appear in sales training, where people learn you can't use the same pitch on everyone because people "hear" in different ways and "listen" for different things.

Which brings us to today's lesson: the four personalities that reside in every mind.

■ Your four sets of ears

Imagine you have four sets of ears. I'll leave the exact mental image of that up to the individual. I see *my* four ears clustered like satellite dishes on each temple.

Each set of ears listens and responds to a different set of stimuli.

1) One set responds to other people. We are a species; we interest each other. We share emotions. We're responsive to others, their warmth, their smiles, their stories, their greetings. We want to help. We like to nurture. We seek community. (I'm talking in general.

Results may vary, person to person.) We call this particular set of ears your AMIABLE side.

2) A second set of ears responds to anything new. These ears plead, "Please, tell me something I *don't* know!!!" They are addicted to the new. They burn for the new. They crave the new. The different. The unique. The only. The urgent. The desperate. "Surprise me!" these ears shriek. Creativity pundit Sean Kernan reveals this shocking(ly wonderful, from a marketer's viewpoint) neurobiological discovery, "Our brains notice and respond to what is new. Not what is interestingly new or significant, but new in any way at all." We call this set of ears your EXPRESSIVE side.

3) Your third set of ears is skeptical. If I had any business theorizing about brain evolution (which I don't), I'd premise that this is a very primitive set of ears, a set that's been wary from the start. We didn't become such a hugely successful species by being gullible. We're suspicious. Sudden movements startle us. We're quite untrusting by nature, and our culture tells us that's a good thing, a safe thing. Our court system says, "Innocent until proven guilty." Our hearts say the opposite, as kind of a low-level default. We're cautious by nature. We call this set of ears your SKEPTICAL side.

4) Your final set of ears only wants to know what to do next. These ears have heard enough. They're

ready to act. "Tell me what to do next," they say, almost impatiently. Go, go, go. Make it obvious. Make it convenient. This set of ears we call your BOTTOM-LINER side.

When you speak to all four sets of ears in your materials, you give yourself four chances to hook the reader's interest, no matter which happens to predominate at that moment. Your messages will...

• Glow with humanity and heart ... and attract the Amiable side of your audience.

• Radiate news value and urgency ... and bring the Expressive side of your audience running.

• Anticipate and answer the predictable objections ... and allay the doubts that eat at the Skeptical side of your audience.

• Never forget to tell people exactly what you wish they'd do next ... so the Bottom-Liner side of your audience can easily respond to your appeals.

14

What the Amiable Side Responds To

Does your newsletter include photos of smiling faces? Do your appeal letters tell stories about the people you've helped? If so, you've done well. Faces and anecdotes are two of the best ways to appeal to the Amiable side of your audience.

Even without reading a book like this, fundraisers instinctively understand the need for Amiable content. They've heard the mantra a hundred times: People give to people. Fundraisers also know that statistical evidence, while important, has limited penetrating power. To reach the heart and give it a good squeeze, you have to "put a face" on the problem.

■ The eyes have it

Go to the magazine aisle in a big bookstore and stare at the covers. You'll soon notice that many of the covers stare back.

No coincidence: publishers know that eye contact has a powerful effect. It can draw a shopper in, compellingly, almost involuntarily, like some "tractor beam" in an outer space movie.

Smiling faces speak to the Amiable side of prospective donors from the gift reply envelopes that Sunshine Cottage (San Antonio, Texas) slips into every newsletter.

German researcher, Dr. Siegfried Vögele, verified this effect in the 1980s. In his Munich laboratory, he proved that eye contact is pretty much irresistible. When you're offered a page with staring eyes, you *will* stare back. Something in your brain requires it.

Incidentally, that soulful stare doesn't have to be human. Animal eyes work well, too.

Eye contact is profoundly Amiable while at the same time exerting a magnetic pull on your readers' attention. But let me point out the obvious: eye contact *only* works if the reader can actually *see* the eyes nice and big. If the faces in your newsletter are printed as small as raisins, the benefits of eye contact are lost.

■ Anecdotes: A mental picture is worth a thousand words

The fastest way I know to explain what you do and why it matters is to insert in someone's mind a scene from a life.

In 23 words I can tell you *more* about the accomplishments of a charter school that uses music to teach the A-B-Cs and the 1-2-3s to kids who have had a tough time in school ... than I can with a *thousand* words about the school's pedagogical foundations and its vital statistics to date. Submitted as evidence, my favorite anecdote:

"This girl, when she entered our third grade, she couldn't spell 'cat.' By the end of the school year, she could spell 'Tchaikovsky.'"

Me, with my two college degrees from a fine Ivy League institution, had to check the dictionary to spell Tchaikovsky correctly in this paragraph. So, needless to say, I'm impressed by what this school did for this child. I also happen to know that the third grade is a critical frontier for children in school. If they don't succeed by the third grade, they're liable to have classroom difficulties forever and are far more likely to drop out.

In 23 words, this charter school has convinced me that they are saving lives.

Anecdotes are like a bullet to the brain. Only *this* bullet is a *good* bullet, exploding into a little mental picture of a happy child spelling T-c-h-a-i-k-o-v-s-k-y.

■ Anecdotes make complex issues easy to understand

Anecdotes are the common coin of human experience.

Once, our ancestors gathered around campfires to hear tales that taught important skills and added to the community's body of knowledge.

Today, fundraisers use anecdotes as micro-documentaries that can instantly interest, educate, and inspire strangers.

We live in a world of complex issues. Yet I can understand *any* issue instantly, no translation or special background necessary, as long as the issue is revealed through an anecdote. Reporters love to start articles with anecdotes for that same reason. Here's a quick, typical example from *The Wall Street Journal* (John Carreyrou, writer):

"Eileen Bloom, a retiree who lives in the lakeside town of Sebring, Fla., has long ordered her medications from Canada, saving up to 50% on her prescription-drug bills. But twice in the past nine months, her medicine hasn't arrived. Ms. Bloom, who suffers from diabetes, is one of tens of thousands of Americans whose drugs have been seized by U.S. Customs and Border Protection."

I get it. I see. In just three sentences, the writer has informed me of an emerging policy beef between U.S. Customs, which backs Big Pharma in its fight to stem cheaper, imported meds; and Congress, which has heard thousands of complaints from constituents like Eileen Bloom.

As a tool for persuasion, an anecdote can easily accomplish as much as a lengthy essay ever will, only far faster and more memorably.

15

Anecdotes Bring Your Successes Vividly to Life

Anecdotes in the service of fundraising come in many shapes and sizes, some no more than a few words long. They all share a goal, though: to bring to life in the reader's mind a picture of success. *Telling* people that your program works is nice. But *showing* them that it works, in the intimate theater of their very own heads, is far more powerful. Here are some ideas to bring your successes to vivid life for the reader:

• There's the *"before-and-after"* anecdote. In the preceding chapter, the Tchaikovsky girl's story of academic triumph is that kind of anecdote. *Before:* she was a classroom left-behind. *After:* she was a classroom champ. Here's another before-and-after example, from a case statement:

"Every year more than 3,000 Providence

public school students face some kind of learning crisis that could end their chances of a successful school career. And then one of our volunteer tutors walks in the door." (Volunteers in Providence Schools)

• A twist on the before-and-after formula is the *"now-and-what's possible"* anecdote. This anecdote conveys your vision and invites participation. It has a built-in call to action. Here's an example from Literacy Volunteers of Massachusetts:

"Nearly 880,000 adults in Massachusetts lack functional literacy skills. That means that they can't complete job applications or read newspapers, road signs, or medicine labels. But you can help." Now *there's* a vivid mental picture: someone in a bathroom somewhere, staring at a prescription bottle, not knowing what it says. *But I can help*, I remind myself.

• *Testimonial* is often anecdotal in nature (it describes a situation in someone's life) and can offer proof that a program has worked. *This* testimonial appeared in the Calgary United Way newsletter alongside a photo of mother and child:

"I believe that if I hadn't had SOFIA House, my son and I would not be alive today."

A totally persuasive endorsement – in a mere 18

words.

• Just as persuasive is *"look-at-the-lives-you've-contributed-to"* material. Saint Mary's University of Minnesota inspired prospective donors with a speedy, little booklet called "Profiles - Your gifts at work." The booklet profiled six students who'd received assistance from various endowed and annual scholarship funds. The profiles were short and sweet. Each consisted of a beaming close-up photo; a statement from the student about how much her or his scholarship meant; and a brief, breezy, bulleted backgrounder that included major, minor, favorite professors, volunteer activities, and last but not least "post-SMU plans."

One young woman's intentions: "Politics and the Oval Office." I know *I'm* impressed. People want to be on the winning team, people including donors.

• Then there's the *"Surprise!"* anecdote. The Surprise! anecdote overturns expectations. It has a very simple formula, enshrined throughout comedy as well as journalism. It's a formula that hooks not only the Amiable side of the personality but also the Expressive; a two-fer.

Here's how it works: You point the reader in one direction — then you head the opposite way.

On the next page is a first-rate example that ran as a headline in *The New York Times*:

Help for the Hardest Part of Prison: Staying Out

I confess: "Staying Out" wasn't my first guess (or my 100th), so this caught my eye. Surprise me, and I'm yours. In another example, from the Housatonic Youth Service Bureau, the Surprise! anecdote foreshadows doom – yet delivers salvation.

"For an agency made necessary by drug and alcohol abuse, teen pregnancy, child depression, youth unemployment, truancy and dropping out, family violence, runaways, homelessness, and petty crime ... we're remarkably happy. Must be all the changes we see in the people we help."

The zig: an intense litany of serious trouble. The zag: an organization happy because it has clearly improved its community by helping individuals and families overcome their demons and dangers.

16

What the Expressive Side Responds To

The Expressive side of the reader's mind craves (demands, expects, adores, and responds to) news. The Expressive side persists in pleading: "Tell me something I don't already know about something I care about."

Nothing could be easier. "Did you know," the Southwest Mental Health Center (San Antonio, TX) asks, for instance, "that many people would rather tell employers they committed a petty crime and served time in jail, than admit to being in a psychiatric hospital?"

A dose of news – in the first paragraph of an appeal letter, on the home page of your website, on the front page of your newsletter, or wherever else eyes happen to land – causes *more* people to pay *more* attention.

But here's some bad news from me to you: *many nonprofits remain "news-challenged."*

If I could sweep across America's nonprofits like the angel of death, eradicating any donor newsletter with no real news value, I swear 90% of them would disappear. Burst into flames. Burn to ashes. Blow away as if they'd never existed.

They call it a "news"-letter for a reason.

It should surprise me, delight me, shock me.

It should never BORE me. BORING me does NOT activate the expressive side of my personality, the side that responds to the new.

Bore me; smother me with "happy talk" (predictable, safe, overcooked corporate-speak); tell me nothing I couldn't already guess or assume or presume or know; and I promise I *will* find better things to do than read your donor newsletter.

Many so-called newsletters in all fairness should be called "old"-letters instead, since donors could have predicted every word.

And don't even get me started on donor newsletters that devote the front page (the most important journalistic real estate you own) to a "Letter from the desk of the executive director." Ninety-nine out of a hundred such letters I've read (and I've read many times that number) are dreadful, a form of written sleeping gas with the power to put donors down instantly.

■ What is news?

That's simple: news is merely information that was 1) previously unknown to your readers; and 2) of special interest to them, because they care about a certain issue. For example...

• Things happen in your organization all the time: "Daring new program promises to cut teen pregnancies in half, but challenges loom."

• Lives change thanks to your work: "Once-homeless mom now succeeds as entrepreneur."

• You're witness to emerging trends: "Soaring real estate market floods shelters with priced-out working poor."

• You see problems long before the public does: "Fifty different languages spoken at home turn city's classrooms into towers of Babel."

• You know things that fascinate your particular supporters: "Ten garden flowers that butterflies can't resist."

You're already swimming in worthwhile news, I promise you. Just remember to talk about it.

17

Newsletter Story Ideas: A Checklist

As a newsletter editor, you'll sometimes feel like you're stranded on a desert island, without a good story idea anywhere in sight. Actually, you're swimming in a sea of material, if you know where to look. Here are 18 ready-made story ideas to choose from, for your donor newsletter:

1) *Program stories.* Pick a program, any program. What has it accomplished lately? Is it growing, shrinking, updating, changing in any way? Do you have handy an anecdote that reveals how successful the program has been or can be? If it's a new program, what made you think it was worth doing in the first place? What are your hopes for the program? Talk about why the program MATTERS, not so much about how it works.

2) *Tips.* As specialists in your field, you have a unique body of knowledge. Some of it might be helpful to others. "The 10 Warning Signs of Childhood Depression." "A Dozen Things You Can Do Today That Will Save the Environment Tomorrow." "Is a Charitable Remainder Trust Right for You? A Checklist From an Expert."

3) *Previews and reports.* What's ahead? What are the latest findings from the authorities? "Looking at Next Year: Where We See Healthcare Headed." "New Urbanists Meet to Plan City of the Future: Will You Want to Live There?"

4) *Client case histories.* Show how your programs have changed individual lives for the better. And don't go all "happy face." Include conflict, tension, doubt, and obstacles, as well as triumph: it makes far more interesting reading.

5) *"Staff are people, too" stories.* What are the people on the front lines really like? Do their personal histories reinforce the credibility of your organization? "New Director of Projects Learned Her Business Building Bridges in Southeast Asian Jungles."

6) **Milestones.** "How 46 Donors Celebrated Our 20th Anniversary: Making $20,000 Gifts in Their Wills." "What We've Accomplished (Thanks to You, Our Donors) In the Last Five Years: A Timeline."

7) *Research and development.* What's coming down your pipeline? The world is ever changing: What programs are you planning to meet new demands?

8) *Publications.* What do you have to offer? Guides, brochures, checklists, white papers, reports, talking points, PowerPoint presentations, downloadable PDF files, an e-newsletter, information on your website: anything a donor, prospect, or client might consider useful is potential news.

9) *How-to pieces.* What do you know how to do that a reader might be interested in? "Listing Your Historic Home on the National Register: Easy To Do, If You Do It Right." "How to Lose 20 Pounds in Two Months the Safe and Sane Way, Without Feeling Hunger Pangs."

10) *Financial news.* People are surprisingly curious about your finances. If for no other reason, openly discussing your financial information signals donors that you have nothing to hide, that you've been wise stewards of their cash contributions. Skepticism about nonprofit business practices has never been higher, polls find. Fight back with transparency: lift the veil on how you spend your money. A good practice: in every issue of your donor newsletter run a pie chart that shows the breakdown of your expenses (assuming, of course, that your administration and fundraising costs are within reasonable standards).

11) *Photos with captions.* And never without a caption. Because many "readers" *only* read easy, brief items of text such as captions and headlines. Your captions are a major opportunity to slip in information.

12) *Columns.* In the preceding chapter I disparaged the "Letter from the executive director's desk" convention. But only because these letters usually land on the front page, a prime position they seldom merit. But letters from the ED *do* have their place. They can be a from-the-heart, me-to-you behind the scenes look into the most pressing issues facing the organization, for instance. Other types of columns include "Frequently Asked Questions," "Q&A," "Myths & Facts," "A donor talks about why she gives," "Letters," "Heard on the blog," or guest columns.

13) *The "Update" story.* Here's a perfect example of an update story from the Ducks Unlimited Canada member magazine: "The West Nile Virus: One Year Later." Ducks Unlimited Canada *owns* this story. Their mission: preserving the wetlands needed by migratory waterfowl, yet now there's a complication: a fatal disease lurks in these very same wetlands. Stay tuned.

14) *The "Did you know?" story.* These reveal surprising, relevant facts. This cover item from the Conservation Law Foundation's newsletter, for instance: "On August 15, 2003, as over 100 power plants remained shut down on the second day of the Northeast's massive blackout, visibility increased by

as much as 20 miles because the concentration of light-scattering particles caused by sulfur dioxide emissions was reduced by 70 percent." In less than 50 words, the donor's reminded poignantly of what the fight's really about: healthier air.

15) *Press releases.* If you think it's news to the outside world, then it's likely to be news to your donors as well.

16) *News about you.* If you attract media coverage, draw attention to that in your own newsletter. It can help build your organization's image and reputation.

17) *History.* A timeline, for instance, can be the best, fastest way to show a long record of steady growth and achievement, something that attracts many donors.

18) *Offers.* Tours, special events, classes, invitations to sign up for an e-newsletter: the list of offers you can make is endless. Offers are important, as you learned earlier in the book. If they're good offers, people respond to them, which in turn helps build relationships. Who wouldn't appreciate this offer made by the San Antonio Area American Red Cross in its newsletter: "Are your CDs paying you 1-2%? Would you like a 10% return?"

Due credit and thanks: the preceding checklist is partially based on one created by Robert W. Bly in his Advertising Manager's Handbook.

18

Sorting the Wheat From the Chaff

On a piece of paper create two columns.

Label your left-hand column: "Story ideas."

Label the right-hand column: "Why do they care?"

And who is the "they?" Your donors or prospects or both: those whose attention and interest you solicit in every issue.

Now you're ready to take a preliminary list of story ideas and refine it. In the process some stories will weaken and die. Other will bulk up into strong performers. It all comes down to whether you can find an angle that makes the donor care.

Let's say that in the left-hand column you write: "Interview with our outgoing board chair." An interview like that can go in a thousand different directions, not all productive. But ask yourself – "Why would donors care to hear from this person?" – and suddenly you have laser focus.

• They might care because the board chair was at the beating heart of the organization when critical decisions got made. He or she can discuss the turning points that helped the organization better meet its mission. ("There was that time we turned down a $100,000 grant. We anguished about that for weeks. But it would have ultimately been bad for the organization. Here's why....")

• They might care because the board chair has a well-informed and powerful vision he or she can share with the organization's supporters. ("The next step for our supporters is to get behind an endowment. If we want to be around for sure twenty years from now, an endowment is our best insurance policy.")

• They might care because, like them, the board chair is also a donor. He or she began giving for a very personal reason that other donors could find intriguing, revealing, even inspiring. ("You know, every day on my way to work I'd see homeless vets on the street, begging. And it just tore something up inside me. So I asked around to see who was doing something about the problem, and this organization came up several times. So I called to volunteer.")

If you gain nothing else from a "why would they care" exercise, you will at least end up with some useful questions to ask when you finally sit down to conduct the interview – and that's how quality interviews begin.

Good journalism begins with "reader-centric" questions. What do our readers really want (need, hope) to know? What will be meaningful information for them? What would surprise them?

And don't forget, we are all voyeurs and we are all gossips and we are all peeping Toms, given a harmless opportunity. So turn over the rock. Tell me something I *don't* know.

19

What the Skeptical Side Responds To

Sure, the donor's Amiable side says, "Go ahead. Take a chance. Trust them. Send them a check." But the Skeptical voice is never silent for long. And the Skeptical side is a chorus of doubts:

- Maybe my gift is a waste of money.
- Maybe this charity isn't effective.
- Maybe their mission doesn't matter.
- Maybe they're wasteful.
- Maybe they don't run a tight ship.
- Maybe they're a bunch of la-de-dah do-gooders without a business bone in their bodies.
- Maybe they won't even be here next year.
- I wonder if there's another charity doing the same work, only better?

Heard enough?

Knowing that thoughts like these (admit it: you have them, too) tinkle like wind chimes in our brains, it's smart to play strong offense; and answer objections before they're asked.

■ The most entertaining meeting you'll ever attend

Gather your colleagues, maybe even your board. Budget one hour.

Ask them to list all the bad things they've heard about your organization. Right or wrong doesn't matter. Dig out misperceptions, suspicions, doubts, objections that lurk out there among your various target audiences: clients, donors, the public, reporters.

Also: ask your colleagues to list the top questions that they hear people ask about the organization.

Finally, colleagues: What are the things that strangers never get right about us? What's our best-kept secret?

When the meeting ends, you'll have the basis for a perfect set of FAQs, with answers that seem to anticipate gracefully and honestly the real unspoken questions hovering out there.

Oh, and don't forget to prioritize. If you uncover 30 questions you can answer, pick a top ten.

Your honest, authentic FAQs calm the fears of the Skeptical mind.

20

Honesty and Information: Reassuring the Skeptic

Skeptics need reassurance before they'll act on your behalf. The strongly skeptical include:

• Prospects considering a first gift;
• First-time donors considering a second gift (according to one expert, about 70% of first-time donors never make a second gift; it seems safe to assume that this huge drop-off is in part due to skepticism that went unrelieved);
• Donors of modest gifts who are thinking about increasing their giving;
• Anyone thinking about leaving you a bequest;
• Reporters.

Reporters are an interesting special case because we have recent research on their habits. Polls reveal that the first place today's reporters go to learn more about your organization is your website. They don't call first. They go to your website for background on your mission, your history, your current operations, your finances, your staff and board, your accomplishments.

This habit offers you a terrific opportunity to make a great first impression. And it's not just reporters prowling your website: anyone with access to a computer can (and will) anonymously assess your organization online. Take advantage of the opportunity to shape their perceptions.

■ What FAQs are for

FAQs (Frequently Asked Questions) are an Internet convention. In your FAQs, web visitors expect to find answers to their foremost doubts. They don't expect to find answers to fake questions like "How do I give more money to you?"

FAQs calm donor jitters; correct misperceptions; challenge falsehoods; overturn wrong assumptions; reassure; help you brand your organization as trustworthy, honest, sincere, humble, worthwhile, thoughtful, and visionary.

■ Required FAQ for donors: Fundraising efficiency

Take a lesson from the United Negro College Fund website, and publish something similar to their "Fundraising and efficiency facts...." Every nonprofit organization should have this particular FAQ, and talk about how efficient your fundraising activities are.

You might also mention that the Better Business Bureau Wise Giving Alliance has established a "best practice," that a nonprofit should spend no more than 20 percent of its income on administration and fundraising. The other 80 percent goes to program expenses.

Here are sample items from the UNCF website:

• UNCF maintains a low cost ratio of only 17.6 percent of total revenues – 7.8 percent for administrative costs and 9.8 percent for fundraising.

• Both *The Non-Profit Times* and *The Chronicle of Philanthropy* rank UNCF among the top 10 charitable educational organizations in the country.

• Approximately 92 percent of students attending UNCF member institutions require financial assistance.

• Fifty-nine percent of students attending UNCF member institutions are from families with a gross income of less than $35,000 and roughly half of UNCF students are from single parent households.

Do the easy thing: search online to see how organizations similar to yours deal with the issue of fundraising efficiency. Simply type into your search engine a cluster of key words such as "FAQ fundraising efficiency child family service." You'll be amazed (and probably even inspired) by what pops up in such a search.

Or limit your search to just the key words "fundraising efficiency." You'll get an eyeful of how various watchdogs, from Charity Navigator to the American Institute of Philanthropy to magazines like *Forbes* rate charities on this often sore subject.

■ Testimonial: The medicine that instantly soothes ordinary cases of "the doubts"

Credible testimonial leaps tall doubts in a single bound. Use testimonial often, everywhere. Testimonial quickly switches off garden-variety, low-grade skepticism.

"We were down to one meal a day in our family. Then the food bank found us." – *Single parent of two youngsters*

"The Foundation answered all my questions about remainder trusts, quickly, in plain English, and without a hint of pressure. It was a great pleasure." – *Philanthropist-to-be*

"My child was having so much trouble, I doubt he'd have stayed in school. The volunteer tutor made all the difference. And I know what getting an education will mean for my child." – *Parent*

"New England's Great Zoo." – *The Boston Globe, of Roger Williams Park Zoo; this particular testimonial became the zoo's de facto tagline, repeated in every publication and press release for years, millions of times total.*

■ Lots of information

Bless the Web.

The World Wide Web can now bring within reach of anyone with a computer (most of us, and certainly donors and the press), a public archive of your organization's background materials, conveniently organized for searching, kept on your website at small cost.

An archive is a good insurance policy. It's a defense mechanism when someone really probes.

Information appeases the voracious skeptic. Lots of information. Background, background, background. Reports. White papers. Press releases. Staff bios. History. An illustrated timeline. Raving skeptics will eat these up, like starving rabbits in a lettuce patch.

21

What the Bottom-Line Side Responds To

Let's keep this brief.

Stop selling.
You want me to give. I get it. I'm convinced.
How?
Show me NOW. This instant.
And make it easy!
Don't make me go scrambling around to find it.

That's how your bottom-line personality thinks.

When you make calls to action (which you should, often, as they deepen the relationship by encouraging involvement), give me a way to *quickly and easily* complete the action.

You want a check? Give me an envelope.

You want my email address so you can send "red alert" bulletins? Write me a personal letter and provide a response card. You want me to volunteer? Give me a warm, welcoming human I can call any time. You want me to request your new brochure about bequests? Give me a card I can return, an email address I can write to, a PDF file I can download, and a receptionist who knows what I'm talking about when I call.

22

The Emotional Imperative

Mostly, people give from the heart. The head is a bit player.

We assume just the opposite. In our post-industrial, technologically-enhanced world, we worship reason. We believe that reason, our ability to work our way intellectually through problems, sets us apart as a species and yields huge benefits. And it does.

But reason has surprisingly little to do with decision-making, neuroscientists now know. (Delicious irony there: science proves that emotion, not reason, controls most choices.)

People don't give to your organization because they've made a coolly calculated decision to support you. They give because you've moved them somehow, sometimes in ways that don't sound all that "charitable." Flattery and greed are important emotional triggers, for instance. But, then, so are hope and joy.

Engage people's emotions and the world is your oyster.

People like to feel things. They like to feel good. They like to feel warm. They like to feel proud. They like to feel they've done something useful and important. They also like to have their anger soothed, their fears relieved. And they'll pay to experience those emotional states, even for a few seconds.

The most profitable direct mail and newsletter programs are those that sustain in donors a constant state of emotional tingle. Consider the abundant use of emotional triggers to be a sort of foreplay. For the donor, writing the check completes the act of love.

NOTE: If you're interested in the science behind emotions, a major new field of neurology, go online to learn about the pioneering work of Dr. Antoine Bechara, Dr. Antonio Damasio, and Dr. W. Gerrod Parrott.

23

Emotional Triggers

I had a bracelet made for my wife, Simone. She's a fundraising consultant, and teaches a lot. But she was always forgetting one or more of the emotional triggers (they're called "triggers" because, when pulled, an emotional reaction happens).

So, as an easy reminder, I had a bracelet made with the seven top emotional triggers stamped into the stainless steel links. There are many more than seven emotional triggers, mind you. But these seven are revered – nay, *worshipped* – by the direct mail industry in the United States.

On her wrist Simone wears a bracelet bearing the following words:

- Anger
- Exclusivity
- Fear
- Flattery

- Greed
- Guilt
- Salvation

If she ever has to go to a hospital, what will people think?

■ The Kennedy Center Invites You

Let's see how some of these seven emotional triggers work in real life.

The example below is from a notably successful membership invitation mailed by the Kennedy Center in Washington, D.C. Results were so spectacular that a major trade magazine wrote up the campaign. Here's what the invitation said in large type, right beneath the logo:

You are hereby invited to become a
Member of the Kennedy Center
at a full 20% discount
and gain the special privilege to
purchase advance tickets before the general public
to the finest Kennedy Center presentations.

This is a professionally written money maker. Let me reveal to you the emotional triggers buried in the author's choice of words:

You are hereby invited [*flattery*] to become a
Member [*exclusivity*] of the Kennedy Center
at a full 20% discount [*greed*]

and gain [*greed*] the special privilege [*exclusivity*] to purchase advance tickets before the general public [*exclusivity*] to the finest [*exclusivity*] Kennedy Center presentations.

You might quickly conclude from this example: the more emotional triggers, the better. And you'd be right. But notice, too, how focused the triggers are in the Kennedy Center piece. They operate within a pretty narrow range: *flattery, exclusivity, greed*. They reinforce each other harmoniously, urging the reader toward a purchase decision.

Some emotional triggers lean negative (fear, anger). Some emotional triggers lean positive (hope, compassion). But one thing is certain: there's no shortage to choose from. Researcher W. Gerrod Parrott has isolated 135 different human emotional states, each distinct enough to be instantly recognizable (see Appendix for his list.) A choice of emotions *that* diverse should be more than enough to suit any fundraising occasion.

24

Choosing Your Emotional Twin Set

What's a twin set? In the clothing trade: a matching pair of women's sweaters, a pullover and a cardigan, meant to be worn together.

Fundraising, though, has its own kind of twin set: *emotional* twin sets, a pair of emotional poles. They stand like two poles of a laundry line, with messages strung between them, flapping in the breeze.

Maybe *fear* is one pole, *hope* the other. Somewhere between fear of the problem you're confronting, and hope that you have the solution, a check gets written (see illustration on next page).

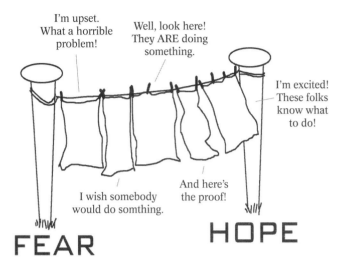

Moving from fear to hope: How a check gets written

■ A common twin set: Fear and hope

I didn't choose fear and hope accidentally. They make an especially powerful combination for many charities: medical research, environmental causes, political campaigns, advocacy efforts. When people feel fear, they wish to relieve it. Desperately so, sometimes. Making a gift to your organization can be the balm of choice.

But there are other twin sets. Heifer International raises a ton of money with the set of *guilt* and *compassion*.

Guilt that we Americans have so much material comfort when others have so little. Relieved by committing an act of compassion: buying a woman in Africa a goat that will improve her family's prospects.

EMOTIONAL TWIN SETS

Catalyzing trigger (often negative, where you introduce the problem)	Calming trigger (positive, often a solution, that offers donors relief if they will act)
Anger: Stirred by photos of abused dogs	**Compassion:** This proclamation appears on the International Fund for Animal Welfare reply form: "Yes, you can count on me for a gift to rescue pets from cruelty, abuse and starvation."
Fear: "No matter how a brain injury is acquired, most survivors and their families find that they have one thing in common: *Life is never the same again.*" Brain Injury Association of Connecticut (BIAC) membership brochure	**Hope:** "That's where we come in." BIAC: "A resource in recovery. A partner in prevention."
Disgust: "Senior Republican Wants to Draft You in the War on Drugs	Outrageous New Bill Makes Americans Choose Between Spying on Their Neighbors and Jail Time" Front page headline in Drug Policy Alliance donor newsletter	**Exhilaration:** "Alliance Supporters Send 8,000 Faxes to Halt Bill" Subhead for same story
Anger: "CHILD ABUSE." Headline of ad for Safe Horizon, "the nation's leading provider of services for victims of violence"	**Optimism:** "Turn Your Outrage Into Action" Subhead for same ad

Continued on next page

EMOTIONAL TWIN SETS

Catalyzing trigger (often negative, where you introduce the problem)	Calming trigger (positive, often a solution, that offers donors relief if they will act)
Guilt: "What will the hungry do on Thanksgiving?" Message (alongside photo of luscious turkey) on Salvation Army appeal envelope	**Relief:** "Yes! I want to help you feed the hungry and poor this Thanksgiving season." Proclamation on reply device
Flattery: "A Circle of Influential Friends Awaits the Pleasure of Your Company" Teaser on envelope for a campaign to attract millionaires interested in philanthropy onto the Rhode Island Foundation's mailing list	**Surprise:** "Welcome ... I hope." First sentence of enclosed letter. (FYI: this "friend-raising" campaign was so successful it became a national model.)

One of the first things I think about on any new project: Which emotional twin sets can we set up to swing our messages between? A single project can exploit several twin sets. These are typical sets: *fear* and *hope, anger* and *compassion, duty* and *salvation, flattery* and *exclusivity*.

25

Answering the Most Important Question: Why Your Organization Matters

A friend introduces you to someone new, mentioning that you work for the XYZ nonprofit. The person asks politely, "What does your agency do?"

"Well," you respond, "we're getting ready to meet a crisis in kids' health care. Most people don't believe it when I tell them. But by 2020, fifty percent of children in the Bay Area will experience some form of childhood cancer before they reach their twenty-first birthday. That's the bad news. The good news is, a cure for those cancers is within reach. Two decades away at most. Our researchers already have the answer. They just need enough money to work out the kinks. The more donors we have, the faster we'll solve this problem."

Elapsed time: 40 seconds, without rushing.

Okay, maybe your organization isn't curing cancer. But your case for support still needs the same elements you see in that response: a dramatic problem, an intriguing solution, news value, urgency, and a critical need that donors can fill. All rolled into a fast, lean speech.

You've probably heard the term "elevator speech." It's a short description of what your organization does, delivered (so the conceit goes) in the time it takes an elevator to travel a few floors: 30 seconds, a minute at most. A good elevator speech doesn't just tumble from your tongue, ready for action. It requires planning and practice.

■ It's not what you do that matters. It's why.

Let's start over. Someone asks, "What does your agency do?" You answer their question. Literally. "We do this. We do that." No surprise. You're an insider. You tend to see your organization in terms of what you do and how you do it: the nuts and bolts of accomplishing your mission.

It's a typical staff obsession: the nitty-gritty of how the work gets done. But donors see things differently. How you do what you do is (take a deep breath) not all that important to the donor. If you could achieve your mission – cure cancer or the feed the hungry –

with a magic wand, donors would be just as happy.

Richard Radcliffe, the world's best-informed authority on legacy giving (he's conducted thousands of focus groups with older donors in the United Kingdom), reports that donors are "staggeringly ignorant" of what charities actually do, even though they make gifts to these same charities.

His research shows that ignorance of the working details of an organization is NOT a barrier to giving. What donors *do* care about is how much you've accomplished.

One often hears fundraisers say, "If we can educate people about our work, they will give." Maybe. Your case is *not* meant to educate your donors about the deep, operational details of your organization. That's like trying to sell cars by handing out owner's manuals instead of sales brochures. Your case *is* meant to inspire prospects and donors so they, in turn, give *through* your organization in order to change the world.

The kind of education that yields gifts, therefore, has to do with your mission, vision, and values: *why* you do the work you do, *why* your organization matters to the rest of the world, *why* you are unique. Keep these distinctions in mind as you hunt and gather information.

People don't need to know how a bulb works to appreciate the light it sheds. People don't need to know how your organization does its work to appreciate what you've accomplished.

119

26

Aren't Sure Why You Matter? Here's a Tip

Get everyone around a table.

Pose this question: "If we were to disappear tomorrow, what would go away that's of real value to the world?" How would your absence affect the community, the target audience, our children, the future? You get the idea. It's a great can-opener. This one question should give you barrels of reasons why you're worth supporting.

27

AIDA: Formula for an Elevator Speech

Advertisers have a simple, reliable sequence for making sales. They call it the AIDA formula. AIDA is shorthand for Attention, Interest, Desire, Action.

The AIDA sequence goes like this.

• First, you grab someone's *attention*. ("There's a crisis in kid's health care!")

• Then, you add *interest*. ("Fifty percent of our kids will get cancer.")

• Next, you stimulate *desire*. ("But we've found a cure.")

• Last, you issue a call to *action*. ("If we have your help, that cure will come much faster.")

■ Using AIDA in the elevator

AIDA is an ideal way to organize your agency's elevator speech.

For instance:

"Our city is breeding a huge social problem that will come due, at huge expense, in just a few years." Assuming the person in the elevator is a taxpayer, you've just grabbed her attention.

"Too few inner-city kids are graduating from high school. Those kids will be virtually unemployable, experts say. They will be mostly condemned to minimum-wage jobs for life. They will be among the chief consumers of tax-supported social services." Pile on the interest.

"But there is a solution." Desire. "We can control this problem so it doesn't come due. Kids who get tutoring help, especially in elementary school, do better in school and graduate at higher rates."

Wrap it up with a vision and a call to action. "We're already helping 3,500 kids head in that direction. We need to help 10,000. Don't worry: we can do it. We're ready. But your help is critical."

Or:

"Nothing prepares you for the thrill of holding an ancient Etruscan sword in your hand. It's perfectly balanced, it's surprisingly light, and I swear it's alive. It feels like it wants to kill." Okay, you have my attention. Now build my interest.

"The Higgins Armory Museum is amazing. There's nothing remotely like it. Here's this world-class collection of medieval and ancient arms tucked away weirdly enough in a small Massachusetts mill city."

Nice surprise. I had no idea such a thing existed nearby. Still, I'm not sure medieval armaments are my cup of tea.

Create desire. "You have kids, right? They will love this place. They can try on a real knight's helmet! You can't imagine how heavy those things are. And bring your camera, too. This is one museum that encourages you to take photos."

Close the sale with a call to action. "Go on a Saturday. The Higgins has experts who put on shows of live sword fighting. First they do it in slow motion with explanations. Then they do it for real; and it's lightning fast. You've never seen anything like this. It's better than the movies!"

28

Making Your Case, Step One: Collect Information

The first step in preparing a persuasive case — whether it's for a new tagline, an appeal letter, a grant application, or a capital campaign brochure — is doing some good old-fashioned homework.

Before you can successfully sell your organization to someone else, you need to fully understand who you are and why you matter. You need to get your hands around your organization and its world.

In short, you need to build a database of information that collects in one place everything you suspect a donor might need to know, would find interesting, or would find persuasive.

Here are the kinds of things you *might* want to review before you start writing your case.

But you probably won't need everything.

I write, on average, one case a month: from a

hospital emergency department, to university endowed chairs, to an urban public school tutoring program, to statewide advocacy campaigns. In one recent 18-month period, I wrote cases for campaigns totaling more than $270 million in requests. This is my comprehensive list of things that come in handy. Sometimes I'll use almost all the stuff in this list. Sometimes I've gotten by with a phone call, an annual report, and a little Internet research.

■ Who we are and what we do sorts of things

- Mission statement
- Values statement
- The organization's history, highlighting its accomplishments
- Descriptions of your programs and services
- Data on those you serve: for instance, membership figures, or the number of participants in your programs
- Proof that your programs and services are worth doing (anecdotal proof, statistical proof, or both)
- Other proof that you're having an impact: statistical evidence of your accomplishments, anecdotes, awards, letters of praise, endorsements, testimonials and so on.
- News clippings about your organization
- All your existing brochures
- Every communication you sent out over the last few years: donor newsletters, alumni magazines, e-

news alerts, invitations, ads, annual reports, direct mail appeals, grant applications and such (they'll remind you of what you've done and what messages you've used in the past)

• Editorials or letters to the editor originating from your organization

• Descriptions of your organization's buildings or other physical holdings

• An overview of your organization's governance: your board, any "friends of" groups, supporting foundations, or advisory groups

• Staffing, including biographical information on management and other key players

• Financial information (an income and expense statement as published in your latest annual report will suffice for many cases)

• Interviews with "key informants." Key informants are those you believe will have an informed opinion about your programs or your vision. You might want to speak with major donors (to ask them why they give), people whom your organization has served (to ask them how you changed their lives), your executive director (to talk about the strategy behind the vision), program directors (to talk about the front line impact), and so on. Interviews take time to schedule and conduct. But they're almost always essential. Some cases require just one; some require a dozen.

• Other research, primary and secondary. Primary research is research you conduct yourself, through surveys, focus groups, or key informant interviews. Secondary research collects useful information originated by others. When you go to the U.S. Census Bureau online, seeking demographic facts about your community, you're collecting secondary research.

■ Where we're headed sorts of things

- Vision statement
- Strategic plan, particularly your goals and objectives
- Information on emerging or increasing needs in your community or constituency
- Your monetary goal for the campaign (if you're campaigning) and what that money will buy

29

Making Your Case, Step Two: Answering the Donor's Three Big Questions

Once you've collected all the background information you think you'll need, the next step is to rake through your foot-tall stack of material, looking for the most persuasive bits. The really good stuff. The stuff with news value. The stuff that's really dramatic, where donors will say, "Wow!"

The goal in step two is to skim the cream: to reduce 20,000 or more words of background material down to just the choicest items — about your campaign, and why it matters to the rest of the world; or about your mission, and how important it is to the rest of the world.

■ Just answer three questions

Ron Arena (of Marts & Lundy, a national consultant to capital campaigns) taught me his minimalist three-question approach to making a case. Simply answer three questions:

1) Why us?
2) Why now?
3) Why you (the prospect)?

Under the first question, *Why us?*, you list your accomplishments, what you're doing to change the world. You also talk about why you're organization is unique, the only, the best. Look for items with news value: fascinating things people don't know about your work. Or mistaken opinions people hold, because you want to correct those opinions. And speak in simple, jargon-free sentences that anyone can understand. If you can't explain yourself without jargon, you're not ready to take your case public.

Under the second question, *Why now?*, you explain why your case is so urgent, why funding can't wait until another day. What's the big rush? What bad thing will almost certainly happen if you don't proceed with your plans? Are you stepping in, in the nick of time, to prevent some imminent harm?

Under the third question, *Why you?*, cue the emotional triggers. Why should anyone care? How are donors heroes when they support your cause? How do they benefit? How is something they love preserved, healed, comforted, or celebrated? How is their fear or anger eased? What hope do you offer?

■ How long should your case be?

Your case can be as short as a tagline. But let's assume you've gone to all this trouble because you want to publish a full-fledged case statement that you can bring to meetings with prospective donors, for your face-to-face solicitations.

How long should such a case be, you wonder?

In my experience, a case you give to donors should be about as long as a medium-sized magazine article. At that length, it will be an easy read, yet can be rich with detail. It should surely be no more than 2,500-3,000 words, unless you don't expect people to read it anyway.

Think of your published case as basically an executive summary of your campaign with some proof attached.

Here are word counts for various published cases that I've done recently, longest to shortest:

• For a university art institute's $5 million endowment: 2,399 words

• For a nationally ranked zoo's $35 million renovation: 2,246 words

• For a philharmonic seeking $7 million in endowment: 2,223 words

• For an urban, public school tutoring program in the $1 million budget range, general case for support: 1,682 words

• For an education advocacy group in the below-$500,000 budget range, launching a major initiative: 1,448 words

• For a regional woman's shelter seeking $7.7 million in construction costs: 1,188 words

• For a regional youth services agency in the $200,000 budget range, general case for support: 936 words

30

Making Your Case, Step Three: Telling Your Story

Okay, you've gathered the data, asked yourself the three big questions, now it's time to tell your story. Here's a model way to do it that's proven effective many times:

1) First, dramatize the problem.

2) Then, present your mission or project as the solution.

3) Beginning to end, speak of the donor as a hero whose gift will help solve the problem.

4) Inside, build conviction and interest. Catalog your real accomplishments, answer objections, give the facts that back up assertions you've made, introduce surprising information, talk about what happens if you don't get to your goal.

5) Ask for the money over and over again. Do not

be shy. If you have a specific dollar amount as a goal, talk about it early and clearly.

This method of telling your story has a number of advantages:

- No risk: it's worked already for many organizations.
- It has a beginning, middle, and end, as stories should. The beginning is the problem/solution. The middle is the proof. The end is the call to action. (Here's an alternative sequence that also works: Start with problem/solution, followed by call to action, followed by proof, followed by another call to action.)
- It keeps your case brief (which is a way to be reader-friendly, always a good thing).
- It is logical. The problem/solution sequence makes inherent sense to most readers. They understand your argument quickly.
- It is emotionally satisfying. The donor stands at the center, the hero who makes all things possible.

■ For example: Us Helping Us

The same story-telling sequence appears in a case statement for Us Helping Us (UHU), a D.C.-based HIV treatment and prevention agency serving African Americans. UHU needed $2 million to renovate an old building into a counseling and treatment center.

1) *Dramatize the problem.* The UHU cover on the next page shows a young black man and woman. Attractive faces, who look readers straight in the eye.

136

WHAT DO YOU IMAGINE IS THE NUMBER ONE KILLER HERE
IN D.C. OF MEN AND WOMEN LIKE THESE?

GUESS AGAIN!
THE KILLER IS HIV/AIDS.

The headline asks, "What do you imagine is the number one killer here in D.C. of men and women like these?" We knew from research that people would typically guess gunshot wound. Exactly what we hoped, because we wanted to surprise them. The real answer: "Guess again! The killer is HIV/AIDS."

2) *Be the solution.* UHU promised to build: "A place where all people – men and women, gay, bisexual, straight – in the D.C. area who are HIV-infected or exposed to risky behavior can get the advice and testing they need to live a longer, healthier life." It would be more than just a clinic. It would be a symbol of resilience and self-reliance: "A place of our own at the corner of hope and health."

3) *Make the donor the hero.* Inside, a chilling list of facts about the epidemic spread of HIV/AIDS in the D.C. area ends in this challenge: "Do you find these facts disturbing? Good. They are. Are you searching for a way to reduce HIV infection here in D.C.? Even better. Time to write a check!"

4) *Build conviction.* Out of eight pages, we devote almost half to listing all the fascinating and unique things UHU does to help reduce and eliminate HIV/AIDS. We make a big deal of their Centers for Disease Control funding. We include a timeline, showing the organization's growth from volunteer-based to professionally staffed. We ease readers into the UHU they DON'T know by first featuring something readers probably DO know: the condom kits that UHU distributes by the tens of thousands in D.C. nightclubs.

5) *Ask for the money.* "Time to write a check!" is only one of several pleas for cash sprinkled through the case.

31

The Smallest Case There Is: Your Tagline

What is a tagline? "A statement or motto that succinctly defines or represents an organization's mission," says one glossary.

What can a tagline do for you? Several useful things. A well-crafted tagline can...

• Explain in a few words why your organization matters;

• Make a promise to your community;

• Hook a newcomer's interest;

• Inspire prospects to become supporters;

• Remind existing donors why they gave in the first place.

A good tagline can be your entire case, all in the blink of an eye.

A tagline usually appears alongside the organization's name. Name and tagline, in fact, work together as a unit, to announce at a glance who you are and what you mean to accomplish. *Tagline* is a fairly modern term; the synonym *slogan* came first. Slogan is an ancient word. It has a deliciously bloodthirsty derivation: "sluagh-ghairm," the Gaelic word for "war-cry" used by Irish and Scottish clans.

Intriguing idea: Your tagline is your war cry. Shout it at the top of your lungs, then charge into the battle for truth and justice.

■ Samples

How do you write an effective tagline? Deliberately. Consider the following taglines and their reasons for being:

1) "Because facts matter in the fight for economic justice." This tagline was written for the Poverty Institute, a think tank that tracks the impact of taxes and legislation on Rhode Island's working poor. The tagline builds on one of the Institute's founding principles: that good information is the basis for fair and effective social policy. The tagline keeps the jargon to a minimum and uses short, direct words like "facts" (instead of "information"), "fight" (suggesting urgency, conflict and action), and "justice" (an ideal the predisposed might respond to).

2) "A place of our own at the corner of hope and health." This tagline was written for a capital campaign conducted by Us Helping Us (UHU), a DC-based HIV/

AIDS clinic and prevention center. The campaign raised money to consolidate the agency's operations, scattered across various rented quarters, into a single, refurbished, UHU-owned facility. The tagline turned one more bricks-and-mortar project into something special, an icon "of hope and health."

3) "Home. There's no place like it." This tagline was the bottom-line message for a well-funded, two-month campaign by HousingWorks RI that persuaded voters to pass a $50 million bond by a wide margin, to fund sorely needed affordable housing for Rhode Island's low- and moderate-income workforce.

■ What's your miracle?

Your tagline explains your mission. But a good fundraising tagline oftens makes a promise, too, a promise that empowers donors: that your gift could work a transformation, maybe even a miracle.

Consider the tagline of the Memphis Child Advocacy Center, "Helping victims become children again." The Center intervenes in cases of child abuse.

I hasten to add that I didn't write this particular tagline. I'm simply an admirer. It is one of the very best I know. It captures in five words the deepest hope of donors: that a child badly battered by sexual abuse, emotional torment, and violence can be restored to health and innocence.

What's *your* miracle promise?

32

Headlines: The Critical Importance Of

It's not just donor newsletters that live or die by their headlines. Not at all. Headlines are *just* as important in your brochures; your annual reports; your websites; your case statement; your press releases; and even your direct mail, if you've used a Johnson Box in your letter or a teaser on your envelope.

Here's why headlines matter: because people skim your materials first, before they read in depth. And what are they skimming? The headlines.

Our hopes die hard. We imagine, we maybe even *expect* (if our sense of entitlement is running a little wild) that people will read everything we write. We want them to study our annual report. We want them to read every precious paragraph in our case statement. We envision them sitting over a cup of freshly brewed coffee, with our direct mail appeal unfolded in front of them, carefully weighing their decision to give.

No.

They browse a little, then go on with their lives. If people don't get the message in your headlines, they're not going to get the message at all. It's a pass/fail situation.

I am my own evidence. Every day, I plow through four daily newspapers looking for items of special interest to my life. This chore takes me no more than 45 minutes. Mostly I just read headlines. I'm equally expeditious with my mail. I read it over a trash basket. Anything that doesn't hook my interest gets tossed within seconds.

Embrace the horror: people receiving your stuff are NOT reading deep. But they do read headlines. So that's where you put your very best mental efforts.

■ How better headlines doubled gift income

It takes about the same time to write a strong headline as a weak one. (I have plenty of experience writing both, so I know.) What differs is the impact on your income.

Weak headlines leave money on the table because donors and prospects remain uninformed as well as unmoved. Faint-hearted headlines do not spur gifts. Strong-hearted headlines make you far more money.

Here's my proof: I know one national advocacy group that recently changed the headlines in its donor newsletter – and doubled their gift income as a result. The editor learned to write strong headlines, bold with drama, emotions, and cheek ... and presto, between one issue and the next, the amount of cash coming back in gift envelopes doubled. But that's not all: the average size of the newsletter-generated gifts was surprisingly large, almost *double* the average gift size from the organization's appeal letters.

A front-page headline from their old newsletter:

From the Executive Director

A front-page headline from their new, improved newsletter:

**Senior Republican Wants to Draft You
in the War on Drugs**

Well-written headlines – in newsletters, appeal letters, brochures, case statements, annual reports, websites – can scream like fire alarms in the minds of those predisposed to care about your mission.

33

Making a Weak Headline Strong

Dr. Mario R. Garcia, an internationally recognized authority on newspapers, offers this prescription in his book, *Redesigning Print for the Web*: "A good headline [has] enticing words, good action verbs, the best possible summary of what the content is about, and, if possible, a surprise or 'hook' that pulls us in."

Here are three headlines from the newsletter of the Audubon Society of Rhode Island (reprinted with permission):

Why Do You Support Audubon?
Survey identifies top two reasons

Your Insurance Policy Provides for Your Long-term Security And Can Protect Critical Habitats

International Coastal Cleanup
Audubon Organizes 1,800 Volunteers
to Clean Our Coast

Are these good headlines? I don't think so. They fail at least two important tests.

The Audubon headlines leave too many questions unanswered. Headlines are a reader convenience. Good headlines let someone quickly browse your contents, to decide if there's anything of special interest to her or him.

Watch yourself read the morning newspaper to see this effect at work. Job #1 for a headline is to summarize the gist of the story. That's the technical function of a headline – to unambiguously explain what the story is about.

The Audubon headlines also don't wield the "good action verbs" Dr. Garcia advises. Instead, the verbs are safe and sluggish: "support," "identifies," "provides," "protect," "organizes." You'll find these same verbs all the time in nonprofit communications. There's a word for them: flaccid. Which means: "Soft, limp, or lacking firmness. Lacking energy or enthusiasm."

Consider two more points.

The first point comes from neurobiology. Human brains, science knows, respond to the new.

Anything new; it doesn't have to be interesting or significant.

Stick in the word "new," and – presto! – your mind pays more attention. (Now you know why advertisers are so fiercely fond of pushing "new.") Also good in headlines: words like "revealed," "secrets," "discovered," "unexpected," "surprise," all signaling "you're telling me something I don't know."

The second point has to do with "donor-centricity."

In an effective donor communications, every headline successfully answers the same question: "Why in the world would the donor care?" Look again at Audubon. Of the first headline, ask this key question: *Why would the donor care that the survey "identifies top two reasons"?* The answer is: We don't know why. Is two some kind of magic number? Are both top reasons important? Time for a rewrite.

Here's the same headline rewritten to satisfy all the criteria, Dr. Garcia's and the donor's:

New Survey Reveals: Land Conservation Ranks #1 On Donors' Wish Lists

Audubon announces drive for war chest to save more land

The rewrite summarizes the gist of the story. Here's a breakdown of the components:

• *New* We have our hook. That tiny word, by itself, always hooks the brain, neurobiology promises.

• *Survey Reveals: Land Conservation Ranks #1 On Donors' Wish Lists* Headlines should only contain the "most important" stuff. The fact that you did a survey isn't important. A dozen surveys are fielded every day. They're as common as weeds. Nor are a survey's raw numbers especially revealing by themselves; they require interpretation to gain meaning. Stop reporting on what you do. Report on why it matters. What matters in a survey is what you *discovered* – that's the real news value.

• *Audubon announces drive for war chest to save more land.* Link the story to donors somehow. Here we point out to them that Audubon needs a "war chest" that will save more land, taking the top interest of those polled (land preservation) and painting it with a charity angle (if you give, we can bring more land under management).

The rewritten headline, as good fundraising headlines should, gives prospective donors a problem they can solve with their gifts.

By the way, that problem donors solve doesn't have to be specific, such as "to cover our electric bill." Most of the time it's better, in fact, if the problem connects to your mission or your vision.

■ A note regarding headline length

The headline rewrite is almost twice as long as the headline that actually ran, 23 words vs. 12. Few are the headlines ("Titanic Sinks") that tell the whole story briefly.

Very often, you'll need more than a few words to summarize the whole story and introduce an angle. Ann Wylie, a national trainer of newsletter editors, recommends that the headline be a summary (eight words or less); and the "deck" (the journalistic term for what civilians call a "subhead") be a comment of 14 words or less.

Those are guidelines, not rules. *The Wall Street Journal* (boasting some of the best headlines in the world) publishes headline/deck combinations that often run over 25 words and up to 40 words. So, yes, keep your headlines as brief as possible. But not so brief they omit the story.

34

Finding the Angle

Consider this headline for a second time. The original, as published:

Why Do You Support Audubon?
Survey identifies top two reasons

Then the donor-centric rewrite:

New Survey Reveals:
Land Conservation Ranks #1 On Donors' Wish Lists
Audubon announces drive for war chest
to save more land

Please note: the original headline has no point of view. The headline merely reported the existence of the survey. It took no position on the survey's results. It had no angle. Instead, the reader presumably would read the entire article and then draw his or her own conclusions undirected by you. There are just two problems: few people read your articles, and even those that do won't necessarily draw the right conclusions.

The angle *is* the story much of the time; simple facts aren't enough. You find your best angle by answering the most important question, *Why would the donor care?* Your mental self-interrogation goes something like this:

"We ran a survey."

> *Why* (you ask yourself) *would a donor care?*

"The survey revealed donors' top concerns."

> *Don't they already know their own top concerns?*

"Individually, sure. But not as a group. If we want to continue attracting gifts from the largest number of donors, our activities have to somehow reflect their top concerns."

> *Fair enough. But let's make it simple to understand. Whittle it down to just one concern. What's the Number One concern?*

Land conservation.

> *Okay. So what emotional triggers relate to land conservation?*

People are interested in conservation because they're afraid all the land will fall into developers' hands and the special places will be lost. So, on the one hand, I'd say fear. And on the other hand, a good bit of anger.

> *What's your emotional twin set? What problem does your organization solve?*

We provide the hope. The negative emotional hooks in the twin set are fear mixed with anger, a potent brew. The positive emotional hook is hope, hope that land will be saved.

> *How will you use the triggers in the headline?*

First, we'll tell them the key result of the survey. That meets the headline's first obligation: to tell the gist of the story. But that same result is also a basic concern: their fear that more land that might be saved, instead could be lost, for lack of a war chest.

> *Great. Now you can write a powerful headline and deck combination. What should go in the deck, do you think?*

In the deck, we will reveal *our* point of view. The truth is, if we had more money, we *could* manage more land. But we can't, because we don't have the resources at this time.

> *Bingo. Now you have an angle a donor might care about. The angle? If you receive more gifts, you'll be able to put more land under Audubon care, should the opportunity arise.*

35

Write For Browsers

Here's a time management tip: focus most of your writing effort on what I call (for lack of a niftier bit of jargon) "the browser level." That's where most eyes will rest first. That's what most people will mostly read. Which makes the browser level your most important writing.

What's in a browser level? It varies from piece to piece. The browser level for an appeal letter, for instance, consists of the following:

- The salutation
- The Johnson Box, if you opted for one
- The opening paragraph (ideally, a single sentence of less than 10 words, experts say)
- Underlined words (use sparingly, to milk the effect)
- Boldface words (ditto)
- Bullet lists (intrinsically easier to skim than copy

set as paragraphs without bullets)
- The closing
- The P.S.

The browser level for a donor newsletter includes:

- Headlines, with decks (a.k.a. subheads) for the most important
- Lead sentences (the first sentence in the first paragraph)
- Bullet lists
- Photos
- Captions
- Pull quotes (a telling or controversial bit of text extracted from the body of the article and given feature treatment)

While the browser level for a website home page might include:

- The search feature
- So-called *persistent* navigation (the navigation elements, such as tabs, that appear on every page)
- Local navigation (the navigation elements for one page only)
- Utilities ("About Us," "Contact Us")
- Things to click on
- Headlines, sometimes with decks
- Shortcuts to popular sections (such as schedules and ticket prices for arts presenting organizations)
- Banners, if you're using them

- Free offers
- Interactive features like "email a friend"

■ The Importance of being Siegfried

Munich, Germany. In the 1980s. Inside his laboratory at the Direct Mail Institute (no joke), Dr. Siegfried Vögele labors. His quest? The secret of eyeballs. *Where do you look when you read?* Dr. Vögele revolutionized direct mail twenty or so years ago. He set up an eye-motion lab. Cameras tracked how people tended to read. His findings were extraordinary.

Among his other discoveries, he noted that eyes involuntarily scooted toward the biggest graphic on a page. Then they quickly skipped around that page, looking at all the things that were bigger, bolder, and briefer.

Those things comprise "the browser level." Since I know that's the really important stuff, I often write my browser level *before* I write any articles. I pack the browser level with emotional triggers. I thread accomplishment, vision, and need everywhere. I rocket-propel my action verbs. I assume that no one will read my articles, but that everyone will read my headlines and other "browser-friendly" tidbits.

Spend your best time on the browser level; that's where it counts.

36

How to Keep Them Reading

Let me insert a reminder here.

You are NOT trying to get people to read.

You are trying to get them to ACT.

Richard Radcliffe again: "Donors are staggeringly ignorant of the charities they support." And that's not a cause for despair. They just don't need to *know* that much to conclude that you're eminently worth supporting.

■ **How keeping them reading improves your fundraising success**

Within 50 words, ideally, you should be able to communicate your need, your urgency, and what the donor can do to solve the problem. Within one headline, one deck, a lead sentence, and call-to-action box, you should be able to pull the trigger.

That said, there *are* real benefits from readers spending minutes (rather than seconds) with your newsletter, annual report, website, special alert, briefing, white paper, or catalog. There are at least three major advantages.

• The longer they spend reading about your accomplishments, your vision, your efficiency, and your reliance on donor participation, the more their loyalty will grow.

• The longer they spend reading, the more likely they are to think about ideas like making a charitable gift in their wills.

• The longer they spend reading, the more lustrous your organization's perceived value will be, as a deliverer of worthwhile, interesting news and information. That will in turn cement your organization's reputation as a leader and authority in its field. Leaders attract bigger gifts.

■ So here's the secret

You keep someone reading in small steps.

And don't expect a total commitment. People almost never read to the end. Assume that no one will read much past paragraph three of whatever you write, for instance; and you will properly armor yourself against disappointment. To keep someone reading that far is easy, though.

Here's the secret: In the very first sentence, tell me something *new* or *interesting*. I've said this before. And

I can't say it enough. People read voluntarily when you surprise them or interest them.

New means tell me something I don't already know, something that I will find *worth* knowing. Or introduce me to someone intriguing, a character in an anecdote.

Interesting means interesting to a *donor*: your accomplishments, your vision and plans, their vital role in your mission, your efficiency.

Beware of assuming your staff's interests are similar to your donors'. Apply the cardinal question to everything you write: *Why would a donor care?* Your staff loves the nuts and bolts of how your programs work. The donor doesn't much care how the machinery runs, but *does* much care about why your programs matter to the community or the world.

Don't try to write fancy, either. Just say things straight out; in simple, jargon-free sentences: subject, verb, object.

Then do it again. And again.

37

Do the "You"

Get yourself a red pen. I myself like the Sanford Sharpie marker with certified nontoxic ink.

Gather at your fingertips a year's worth of your donor communications. Pull from your files your appeal letters, newsletters, any invitations to special events, your annual report. Print out a hard copy of your website's home page, too. You'll want to check that.

Now I'll ask you to conduct the "you" test on all this stuff.

The "you" test is the quickest, surest way I know to judge whether materials are basically "donor ready." And it's dirt simple. I invented this test, and I fully expect to get the Nobel Prize in Usefulness someday. With the red pen in hand, circle each time the word "you" appears in your material – any form of "you": *you'd, you'll, your, you're, yours, yourself, you've.*

Gaze at the results. If you see red circles all over

Dear Ms. Jones,

First, the thanks. *Then,* the invitation.

Thank you from each of us on the board.

You make everything possible. The Women's Fund of Rhode Island is 100% charity funded. You are our investors.

Your support already means a better, more promising life for women and girls across Rhode Island. You've done more than you might realize.

With your gift to the Women's Fund of Rhode Island, you've helped launch a dozen innovative programs that can improve the well-being of our state's women and girls. You've influenced legislative action. You've researched the truth and revealed important new facts about the *real* situation for women and girls in Rhode Island.

Thanks to your help, women's issues are again receiving serious public attention. The *Providence Journal* devoted two days of front-page coverage to the Fund's surprising 2006 poll results regarding women's political behavior in Rhode Island.

Today, we're thrilled to say, we have yet another reason for writing.

We want you to join us.

We'd like to see you inside Simone's Circle.

Simone's Circle is our new legacy society. It is destined to be our most exclusive group ... but the best kind of exclusive. In this small circle you will find *just* those determined to keep their values alive ... forever.

If you believe that the problems of Rhode Island's women and girls *can* find solutions ... as long as someone cares enough to stand up and do something ... consider joining us inside Simone's Circle.

Which, though exclusive, *is* quite easy to join.

To enroll, simply include in your will a charitable gift for the Women's Fund of Rhode Island ... and let us know (we enclosed a convenient card). We will acknowledge your gift immediately and automatically enroll you in the Circle and all its activities. Of course, we will also assure your privacy, if you wish your gift to remain anonymous.

Passing the "you" test with flying colors is this letter to donors, which introduces the legacy society of the Women's Fund of Rhode Island.

the place, you've passed the "you" test.

If you see few red circles and there are large spaces

without any circles, you've failed. Passing the "you" test means you could raise lots of money. Failing the "you" test means you won't.

■ The preeminent "you"

The word "you" has super powers. "You" is the single most profit-generating word in advertising. (Close seconds: "free" and "new.") "You" is glue, too: by itself, it keeps people reading. It is sweet to the eye and ear. Each time the word "you" comes up, we pay a little more attention, as if we'd been personally addressed.

Using "you" often is the easiest psychological trick I can teach you, in your drive to capture fundraising dollars. The word "you" moves oceans of money. Those who use "you" well, do well.

Why does the trick work? I have my own untested, unscientific (i.e., crackpot) theory. I think it's because we're called "you" far more often than we're called by our own names, from our earliest days on Earth. "You, hoo." "Honey, are you ready?" "Hey, you!" "Did you do your homework?"

Over time, our brains develop an autonomic response. Pavlov's dogs had their bells. In English, we have the word "you."

■ Spread "you" thickly on the browser level

You is glue. Have drops of it everywhere the eye might briefly land, particularly in the browser level of every donor communication effort.

38

The Dangerous "And"

"And" can be dangerous to your writing health. It's *way* too easy.

"And" has its purposes, of course. It can be a way of saying, "Oh, one more thing I want to mention."

But "and" is also an invitation to fuzzy thinking, dangling sentences, untrimmed intellectual efflorescence, all flaws that douse readers' interest.

Consider these samples of writing from a university white paper. I've made the "and"s all caps so they're easier to spot:

> The arts merit strong support both because of the opportunities they offer our students in terms of individual personal experience AND intellectual growth, AND because of what a vital arts profile can accomplish for the college AND the community overall.

First, let's check their "readability vital signs." These passages post extremely "reader-unfriendly" scores on the standard measures built into Microsoft Word (search under "readability statistics").

The Flesch-Kincaid "grade level" score is in the red zone, as high as it goes: the 12th grade level, which means this text is impossible to read quickly. The Flesch "reading ease" score is an embarrassing 18 out of a possible 100. If this writer gave any consideration to the reader's comfort, it's not apparent.

And yet....

A simple rewrite, sans some of the ANDs, fixes the flaws.

> The arts deserve our strong support. They offer our students two kinds of opportunities. Students have the chance for intense personal experiences. Plus they'll grow intellectually. The arts also give the college a different national profile. And they add vitality to the community around us.

The grade level now for exactly the same information: 7.5. The reading ease score: 54 out of 100. Not *great,* not by a long shot. But much better – for the reader.

39

Will You Ever Be A Good Writer?

That depends on one thing: How good a self-critic you are.

There's no real need, of course, for you to write all that well or all that much to be an effective fundraising communicator. I'm dead serious. If you can write a decent headline-and-deck combination for your donor newsletter or annual report or website, you're nine-tenths of the way to where you need to be.

Maybe the only real exceptions to the "no real need to write well" rule are direct mail and email solicitations. There, the better you are at your craft, the more money you raise. My advice to direct mail novices: Take two how-to books and call me in the morning. And make one of them Mal Warwick's *How to Write Successful Fundraising Letters.*

But let's say you're like me: You've had a burning

desire to write since you were a child. You want to do it *so* well that people will enjoy reading what you have to say, *so* well that your writing might even persuade them to act. What do you need to know?

■ Tough self-love

We're back at the beginning: How good a self-critic are you?

Writing isn't about writing. Ultimately, it's about interesting the reader and sustaining that interest. In that sense, it's a fairly selfless act. It's not about you at all. It's about the eyes and minds on the receiving end.

Which leads me to rule number one: Stamp out self-indulgence.

Fancy words tickle you? Restrict yourself to ones with the fewest syllables.

Extended metaphors thrill you? Write your tale in as straightforward a manner as you can manage.

Feel that a little digression never hurt? Get to the point.

Eventually, if you practice, practice, practice, you *will* develop your own style of effective writing. And that style might even include all of the above: big, chewy words; metaphorical finesse; cosmic digressions that keep readers enthralled.

But developing a style is step two. Step one is learning to say what you need to say in simple, transparent, speedy prose. The most important question you can ask of any word, phrase, sentence, paragraph, or passage is this: Do my readers really need to hear that?

Someone famously said, "Kill your darlings." William Faulkner, Mark Twain, F. Scott Fitzgerald have all received credit for this handy advice. Translation: Anything you love too much — a phrase, a description, a few paragraphs that are gorgeous by themselves but simply don't play well with the prose around them — is a candidate for a mercy killing.

"Writing is rewriting," everyone says. Deleting words you've fallen madly in love with will hurt at first. But in a good way. And finally it becomes a pleasure because you see your writing improve instantly.

Afterword

I left out a chapter. It's called: on feeling stupid. What was there to say?

But it is very much part of the creative process.

There comes a time when you have enough information. Yet you have no idea what to say.

To pass the time, you sit there, feeling stupid, checking the weather forecast, reading emails, wasting time. Of course, being well raised and responsible, you beat yourself up regarding your lack of progress.

Stop worrying.

Progress *is* happening.

Even though you *feel* stupid, your brain is actually doing some of its very best work while you despair. Your mind is in the midst of digesting what you've fed it. All of this happens in the sub-basement, out of sight, in the mental la-bor-atory (cue lightning flashes). Your subconscious mind is hard at work, sorting, noticing things, looking for that "big idea" that will convince donors to sing Hallelujah.

I can no longer count the times I've popped awake at 4 a.m., the solution to, say, a case statement now, for the first time, clear in my head. It's happened often enough that I sleep with a small notepad and pen handy. And I've learned how to write in the dark.

Preparation is nine-tenths of the work. Once you're well prepared, relax. A great idea will come.

Enjoy feeling stupid while you can. It doesn't last.

Acknowledgments

Many thanks to the organizations whose examples appear in this book and to the people who toil to raise money for worthy causes.

Audubon Society of Rhode Island, Boys & Girls Club of Pawtucket, Ducks Unlimited Canada, EcoLogic, Heifer Project International, Housatonic Youth Service Bureau, HousingWorks RI, Literacy Volunteers of Massachusetts, Memphis Child Advocacy Center, Roger Williams Park Zoo, Saint Mary's University of Minnesota, San Antonio Area American Red Cross, Sierra Club, Southwest Mental Health Center, Sunshine Cottage School for Deaf Children, United Negro College Fund, United Way of Calgary, Us Helping Us, Volunteers in Providence Schools, Women's Fund of Rhode Island.

Special thanks to mentors, colleagues, and friends:

Ron Arena, Robert W. Bly, Lisa Bousquet, Ken Burnett, Kim Butler, Remo Campopiano, Jerry Cianciolo, Sarah Coviello, Nisia Hanson, Steve Herlich, Kris Hermanns, Dianna Huff, Chris Jenkins, Simone Joyaux, Ari Matusiak, Harvey McKinnon, Dave Mealey, Kristine Merz, John C. Meyers, Richard Radcliffe, Jim Rattray, Rick Schwartz, George Smith, Steve Thomas, Mal Warwick, Ryan West, Allen Wong.

APPENDIX

Resources

In my own work as a writer of fundraising and advocacy materials, I've found the following books remarkably helpful:

Advertising Secrets of the Written Word, Joseph Sugarman - Takes you deep inside the mind of consumers.

The Art of Readable Writing, Rudolf Flesch - "The man who taught AP how to write" reveals how to keep a reader glued to the page in this 1949 classic.

Asking, Jerold Panas - Lose the fear.

The Brand Gap, Marty Neumeier - A brief, authoritative guide to what branding really is.

Building Donor Loyalty, Adrian Sargeant and Elaine Jay - The factors behind donor retention. Essential reading.

Confessions of an Advertising Man, David Ogilvy - The wise opinions of a legend who made a fortune in advertising.

The Complete Book of Model Fund-Raising Letters, Roland Kuniholm - A collection of 350+ letters to borrow ideas from.

The Copywriter's Handbook, Robert W. Bly - How to write effective sales copy, an essential skill valuable to fundraisers.

Donor Centered Fundraising, Penelope Burk - "How to hold on to your donors and raise more money," based on six years of research.

Don't Make Me Think, Steve Krug - Before you redesign your web site, read this amazing book.

Don't Think of an Elephant, George Lakoff - How to frame your message and why it matters. A must for advocacy.

Hidden Gold, Harvey McKinnon - The bible of monthly giving.

How to Write Successful Fundraising Letters, Mal Warwick - The best single book I know on its topic. The title says it all.

The Nonprofit Membership Toolkit, Ellis M. M. Robinson - Building a grassroots social change organization, soup to nuts.

Open Immediately! Stephen Hitchcock - Eye-opening "straight talk on direct mail fundraising" from the president of Mal Warwick and Associates.

Raising Thousands (if Not Tens of Thousands) of Dollars with Email, Madeline Stanionis - Here are the answers to a frequently asked question: How does email fundraising really work?

Tested Advertising Methods, John Caples - A revered classic that will change the way you write headlines forever.

Testing, Testing, 1, 2, 3, Mal Warwick - To learn how to test your fundraising direct mail and improve returns.

W. Gerrod Parrott's List of Emotions

KEY: **Primary emotion**
Secondary emotion
Tertiary emotions

LOVE

Affection
Adoration, affection, love, fondness, liking, attraction, caring, tenderness, compassion, sentimentality

Lust
Arousal, desire, lust, passion, infatuation

Longing
Longing

JOY

Cheerfulness
Amusement, bliss, cheerfulness, gaiety, glee, jolliness, joviality, joy, delight, enjoyment, gladness, happiness, jubilation, elation, satisfaction, ecstasy, euphoria

Zest
Enthusiasm, zeal, zest, excitement, thrill, exhilaration

Contentment
Contentment, pleasure

Pride
Pride, triumph

Optimism
Eagerness, hope, optimism

Enthrallment
Enthrallment, rapture

Relief
Relief

SURPRISE

Surprise
Amazement, surprise, astonishment

ANGER

Irritation
Aggravation, irritation, agitation, annoyance, grouchiness, grumpiness

Exasperation
Exasperation, frustration

Rage
Anger, rage, outrage, fury, wrath, hostility, ferocity, bitterness, hate, loathing, scorn, spite, vengefulness, dislike, resentment

Disgust
Disgust, revulsion, contempt

Envy
Envy, jealousy

Torment
Torment

SADNESS

Suffering
Agony, suffering, hurt, anguish

Sadness
Depression, despair, hopelessness, gloom, glumness, sadness, unhappiness, grief, sorrow, woe, misery, melancholy

Disappointment
Dismay, disappointment, displeasure

Shame

Guilt, shame, regret, remorse

Neglect

Alienation, isolation, neglect, loneliness, rejection, homesickness, defeat, dejection, insecurity, embarrassment, humiliation, insult

Sympathy

Pity, sympathy

FEAR

Horror

Alarm, shock, fear, fright, horror, terror, panic, hysteria, mortification

Nervousness

Anxiety, nervousness, tenseness, uneasiness, apprehension, worry, distress, dread

The Triple Crown
for Nonprofit Boards

Each can be read in an hour • *Quantity discounts up to 50 percent*

Fund Raising Realities Every Board Member Must Face
David Lansdowne, 112 pp., $24.95, ISBN 1889102105

If every board member of every nonprofit organization in America read this book, it's no exaggeration to say that millions upon millions of additional dollars would be raised.

How could it be otherwise when, after spending just *one* hour with this gem, board members everywhere would understand virtually everything they need to know about raising major gifts. Not more, not less. Just exactly what they need to do to be successful.

Asking Jerold Panas, 112 pp., $24.95, ISBN 1889102172

It ranks right up there with public speaking. Nearly all of us fear it. And yet it is critical to our success. Asking for money. It makes even the stout-hearted quiver.

But now comes a book, *Asking: A 59-Minute Guide to Everything Board Members, Staff and Volunteers Must Know to Secure the Gift*. And short of a medical elixir, it's the next best thing for emboldening you, your board members and volunteers to ask with skill, finesse … and powerful results.

The Ultimate Board Member's Book
Kay Sprinkel Grace, 114 pp., $24.95, ISBN 1889102180

Kay Sprinkel Grace's perceptive work will take board members just one hour to read, and yet they'll come away from *The Ultimate Board Member's Book* with a firm command of just what they need to do to help your organization succeed.

It's all here in 114 tightly organized and jargon-free pages: how boards work, what the job entails, the time commitment involved, the role of staff, serving on committees and task forces, fundraising responsibilities, conflicts of interest, group decision-making, effective recruiting, de-enlisting board members, board self-evaluation, and more.

Emerson & Church, Publishers

INDEX

Copies of this and other books from the publisher
are available at discount when purchased
in quantity for boards of directors or staff.

Emerson
& Church
PUBLISHERS

Other Books of Interest by Emerson & Church

Raising Thousands (if Not Tens of Thousands) of Dollars with Email

by Madeline Stanionis • Emerson & Church, Publishers • $24.95

After reading the title of this book perhaps you're saying, "Sure, Red Cross and UNICEF can raise tons of money with email, but my agency isn't a brand name. You're telling me I can do the same!?"

Well, no. Author Madeline Stanionis is President of Donordigital, not Pollyanna. But what she is saying is that you can have surprising success if you approach email fundraising with a measure of intelligence and creativity.

Generously dispensing advice and insider tips, Stanionis reveals precisely what you need to do, step by step, to raise substantial money with email.

Over Goal! Expanded and Revised 2nd Ed.

by Kay Sprinkel Grace • Emerson & Church, Publishers • $24.95

To conserve or to change? With all due respect to the Prince of Denmark, that is the question ... as far as today's fundraising is concerned.

Do we cling to traditional practices even when their foundation is compromised, or do we forsake "tried and true" ways so as to woo a new generation of donors demanding different approaches?

Clearly the answer, according to Kay Sprinkel Grace, is ... both. And knowing what to conserve and what to change is the essence of her expanded and revised 2nd Edition of *Over Goal!*

In its first incarnation, *Over Goal!* attained classic status (more than one sage called it "the new bible of fundraising"). But now Grace has taken a scalpel to her original and invigorated it with 12 new chapters while updating trends and figures.

Raising $1,000 Gifts by Mail

by Mal Warwick • Emerson & Church, Publishers • $24.95

Whoever heard of raising $1,000 gifts (not to mention $3,000, $4,000 and $5,000 gifts) by mail? That's the province of personal solicitation, right? Not exclusively, says Mal Warwick.

With carefully selected examples and illustrations, Warwick shows you how to succeed with high-dollar mail, walking you step by step through the process of identifying your prospects, crafting the right letter, the right brochure, the right response device, and the right envelope.